Totally Unofficial:

RAPHAEL LEMKIN
AND THE GENOCIDE CONVENTION

SERIES EDITORS
Adam Strom & the Facing History and Ourselves Staff

PRIMARY WRITER
Dan Eshet

With an Introduction by Omer Bartov, John P. Birkelund
Distinguished Professor, Brown University

CREDITS AND PERMISSIONS

This publication was made possible in part by funds granted by the Charles H. Revson Foundation. The statements made and views expressed, however, are solely the responsibility of Facing History and Ourselves.

He had no money, no office, no assistant. He had no U.N. status or papers, but the [U.N.] guards always let him pass. . . . He would bluff a little sometimes about pulling political levers, but he had none. All he had was himself, his briefcase, and the conviction burning in him. We would say to him: Lemkin, what good will it do to write mass murder down as a crime; will a piece of paper stop a new Hitler or Stalin? Then he put aside cajolery and his face stiffened. "Only man has law. Law must be built."

A. M. Rosenthal, *A Man Called Lemkin*

TABLE OF CONTENTS

FOREWORD

Adam Strom

Director of Research and Development, Facing History and Ourselves

How many times have you seen people in need but chosen not to get involved? Maybe you did not know how to make a difference, or you averted your eyes with the hope that somebody else would make it stop. All of us, if we were honest with ourselves, have been bystanders. Often thinking about when and how to get involved takes place within a split second and by the time we are ready to act, the opportunity to respond is lost. One reason people may not get involved is a belief that it's best to mind their own business. Yet, many of us learned from parents, friends, schools, or religious leaders that there are times when it is a moral imperative to help people in trouble. Sometimes after people miss an opportunity, they find themselves replaying those split seconds dilemmas over and over again in their minds, thinking about what they could or should have done, or what actions they would take if faced with that situation again. History is full of stories about individuals and groups who have faced similar choices.

Facing History and Ourselves teachers and students explore those moments, both in history and in their lives, with the hope of helping students think about the

> **How many times have you seen people in need but chose not to get involved?**

responsibility of an individual to society, which is the essence of global citizenship. In their boldest dreams, many students hope to find a solution to some of the world's most daunting problems: violence, disease, and discrimination. But little attention is given to educating students about the process and the politics of making change. Often students learn little about the people who have dreamed big and made a difference. When students do learn about them, they are often presented as larger-than-life heroes. Students feel that they can never be like these heroes. Through an initiative called *Choosing to Participate* (including conferences, exhibits, study guides, workshops, and lesson plans), Facing History and Ourselves strives to help students understand that they, too, can make a positive difference in the world.

This case study about Raphael Lemkin is the first of a series of *Choosing to Participate* case studies that Facing History and Ourselves is developing about people from all across the world and in all walks of life who chose to participate. These case studies will illuminate what the co-chair of the Facing History and Ourselves and Harvard Law School Project Martha

Minow calls the "levers of power"—the tools available to individuals and groups seeking to fight hatred, prevent genocide, and strengthen democracy. "Levers," she explains, can be used to exert pressure to direct and redirect power, and to advocate. The avenues through which people can exert power and create change include formal legal and political institutions; nongovernmental organizations; the media; and social movements at the local, state, national, and international levels. Lemkin's story, like all of the case studies in this series, will follow a journey: he was outraged at injustice; struggled with different solutions; worked with other people and institutions; had ups and downs; made an impact; and left a legacy on which for all of us to build.

It is appropriate for Facing History and Ourselves to begin this series with a study of Lemkin. It is only because of his vision—supported by others—that we have a word, genocide, to describe the brutal destruction of ethnic, religious, or cultural groups. Lemkin understood that the problem of mass murder was not new, but he believed that people lacked both law and language to help them prevent future atrocities. In particular, Lemkin's story connects two histories that Facing History and Ourselves teachers and students study, the Armenian Genocide and the Nazi Holocaust, to the dilemmas all people face when they witness mass murder and genocide today.

While Lemkin was able to coin a word and convince diplomats at the United Nations to pass the Convention on the Prevention and Punishment of the Crime of Genocide, his work was not complete upon his death. The job of lobbying governments across the world to ratify the convention was left to ordinary people; many of them never knew Lemkin. Sadly, Lemkin's work remains unfinished; genocide continues to this day and it is up to ordinary people across the world to use the legal and political tools that Lemkin created to not only prosecute perpetrators of genocide, but also to work towards fulfilling Lemkin's hope of ultimately preventing genocide from happening.

This case study highlighting the story of Raphael Lemkin challenges all of us to think deeply about what it will take for individuals, groups, and nations to take up Lemkin's challenge. To make this material accessible for classrooms, this resource includes several components: an introduction by genocide scholar Omer Bartov; a historical case study on Lemkin and his legacy; questions for student reflection; suggested resources; a series of lesson plans using the case study; and a selection of primary source documents.

This case study and the accompanying lesson plans were a dynamic process that involved many people including Facing History and Ourselves staff, editors, and scholars. They deserve to be recognized. Margot Stern Strom, inspired by the work of Samantha Power and Martha Minow, insisted that the Lemkin case study be the first in this series. Dan Eshet worked tirelessly on draft after draft to get both the history and the language right. Marty Sleeper and Marc Skvirsky made significant contributions to this work. Brown University historian Omer Bartov read drafts and offered his insights. Jennifer Gray played a vital role as a research assistant on this project— doing everything from correcting footnotes to finding photos and securing permissions. Nicole Breaux helped to manage the project. Robert Lavelle provided oversight for publication. Elisabeth Kanner drafted the lesson plans that accompany the case study. Carol Barkin and Cynthia Platt both served as editors, and Kathleen Branigan designed the guide.

INTRODUCTION

Omer Bartov
John P. Birkelund Distinguished Professor, Brown University

Genocide, the intentional destruction of ethnic or national groups, has been part of human history for millennia. But since the late nineteenth century, its nature and scale have dramatically changed. This was largely because of several related factors. First, the invention of nationalism meant that large numbers of people came to be categorized as belonging to the same group, whether because of their ethnic or racial origins, or because of their social and political affinities. This meant both voluntary and enforced inclusion of people in the new nation, and often violent exclusion of other groups from it. Second, the political consequence of nationalism was the emergence of the nation-state, that is, of states that defined themselves as the political expression of a certain nation. These new nation-states were very different from the old monarchies or empires, whose identity was defined by their rulers and whose populations, often of varied religious, ethnic, and racial origins, were merely the subjects of their monarchs and emperors.

Third, the growing interest in science, biology, anthropology, evolution, and the "origins of man," meant that especially Europeans and Americans began to think of humanity as divided into different races with unique and innate, or in-born and unchanging, qualities and characteristics. The late nineteenth century also saw a vast expansion of colonial empires, in which people of European origin came to dominate, exploit, and often destroy large groups of non-Europeans. This increased the feeling among white people that external physiological differences also indicated intellectual and moral superiority and inferiority. Consequently, it was thought that some people, nations, and races, had a right to dominate others, and that some groups were doomed to extinction because of their racial inferiority. Finally, the late nineteenth century saw an extremely rapid expansion in military and industrial technology, along with great improvements in the state's ability to master its resources, control its population, and project power beyond its borders.

The combination of these factors— in what is now known as the age of nationalism, industrialization, modernization, and colonialism—also served to greatly expand the scope of the targeted and intentional destruction of population groups and to legitimize such mass killings and eradication of cultures

> **Genocide, the intentional destruction of ethnic or national groups, has been part of human history for millennia.**

with seemingly sound scientific arguments. This is one crucial element in modern genocide: It is not only more efficient and claims far larger numbers of victims than in the past, but it also presents mass murder as a necessary and legitimate undertaking, and finds support among intellectuals, academics, spiritual leaders, and others who would normally oppose the murder of individuals.

Modern genocide spread from the periphery of the West to its center. Intentional mass murder and eradication of human populations occurred in various parts of the vast colonial empires, such as German Southwest Africa or Tasmania. Other populations, such as the inhabitants of Congo and Native Americans, were subject to exploitation, massacres, and ethnic cleansing that caused millions of deaths and destroyed entire cultures and language groups. On the periphery of Europe, the Balkan Wars against Turkish rule and between the new nation-states that emerged in the region saw widespread massacres of populations defined by ethnicity, race, and religion. The transformation of the multiethnic and multireligious Ottoman Empire into a nation-state based on the notion of Turkish identity culminated in the genocide of the Armenian population during World War I.

World War II brought the evil fruits of nationalism, colonialism, racism, and modern killing techniques and bureaucratic organization into the heart of Europe. The Nazi extermination of the Jews, and mass murder operations against many other groups defined by Nazi ideology as racially inferior, caused the greatest single destruction of lives, property, and cultures in human history. Having wreaked unprecedented devastation in the West, genocide and its related forms of ethnic cleansing and other crimes against humanity again spread out as far as Cambodia in the 1970s and Rwanda in the 1990s, even as it also continued taking its toll on Europeans, most prominently during the wars in the former Yugoslavia.

What are the main constraints on implementing the Genocide Convention initiated by Lemkin and adopted by the United Nations in 1948?

Attempts to put an end to the scourge of modern genocide within the context of the international community came in the wake of particularly violent periods of mass killing. Following World War II and the Holocaust, the new international desire to tackle state-sponsored crimes was demonstrated in the Nuremberg trials (1945–46), the United Nations Convention on the Prevention and Punishment of the Crime of Genocide (1948), and the United Nations Universal Declaration of Human Rights (1948). A similar surge in international legislation came at the end of the Cold War and the mass murders of the 1990s. On one hand, such attempts must be seen as crucial steps on the long road to eliminating genocide. On the other hand, the persistence of genocide to this day reveals the tremendous obstacles that stand in the way of individuals and organizations dedicated to its eradication. The case of Raphael Lemkin, who coined the term genocide and devoted his life to fighting it, is in this sense both uplifting and dispiriting. It illustrates that a single individual can make a difference and change people's perceptions and the conduct of nations. It also demonstrates the limits of individual influence, the constraints of policy, and the "fragility of goodness" (as analyzed by French author Tzvetan Todorov).

What are the main constraints on implementing the Genocide Convention initiated by Lemkin and adopted by the United Nations in 1948? To what extent does this convention and the often scandalous reluctance of its signers to apply it to ongoing genocides illustrate the contradiction between the desire to prevent evil and enforce good and the duty of states to protect the lives and ensure the prosperity of their own citizens? By way of introducing the story of Lemkin and the "invention" of genocide, let us consider the following points:

1. THE GENOCIDE CONVENTION INTRODUCED A CONCEPT of intervention in the domestic affairs of other states that contradicts the most sacred element of international relations,

namely, state sovereignty, according to which states are not allowed to intervene in each others' affairs as long as they are not attacked by them. There is no simple resolution of this contradiction. Insistence on state sovereignty may facilitate domestic genocide; insistence on humanitarian intervention may justify wars of aggression. Hypothetically, only the United Nations can provide a balanced judgment in such cases. But the United Nations is an organization that represents states whose primary responsibility is their own national interest. In most cases they can be expected—as has happened often in the past—to protect state sovereignty and to oppose humanitarian intervention at least on a significant scale.

2. THE GENOCIDE CONVENTION AND THE CONCEPT of crimes against humanity assume that citizens of a sovereign state, obeying the orders of their government and the laws of their state, may at the same time be committing crimes against humanity for which they could be prosecuted and punished. Because genocide is by definition not an individual crime but a large-scale undertaking by an organization, agency, or state, it creates a very different relationship between individual perpetrators and the law than that of conventional criminal cases. Conventional criminals operate outside the law; genocidal perpetrators carry out the orders of superiors, which are often also legally sanctioned by the state. Yet conventional murderers usually kill very few people, while genocidal perpetrators may be responsible for the deaths of hundreds of thousands or

more. Moreover, in genocide, those who organize the killing rarely have any blood on their hands, while those who spill blood are often very low on the hierarchical ladder. In the past, we have seen that states usually get away with murder on a far larger scale than individuals. Most Nazi perpetrators were never tried. Most of those tried were acquitted. Most of those convicted served ridiculously short prison terms. Yet one cannot put an entire nation on trial without destroying it thereby, in a sense, answering genocide with its equivalent.

3. THE GENOCIDE CONVENTION ASSUMES A NOTION of universal jurisdiction, according to which individuals suspected of committing crimes against humanity could be arrested and brought to justice by any nation in which they reside. This is in response to the tendency of genocidal perpetrators to find refuge in countries that were not involved in their actions. Such status of international outcast can best be determined by the International Criminal Court, proposed in the Genocide Convention and only recently established. The problem with such bodies as the ICC is similar to that of the United Nations. On one hand, it can be effective only if it has a strong enforcement agency, which in international relations has often been the United States. On the other hand, it is precisely the agents of such bodies who may find themselves facing charges by the ICC because they will be operating outside the bounds of their sovereign state. Universal jurisdiction can, and has been, abused by political and ideological interests.

Yet without universal jurisdiction, the danger of perpetrators going free, which is one of the main causes for the recurrence of genocide, will remain unresolved.

4. THE GENOCIDE CONVENTION'S CALL FOR INTERVENTION in case of a threat of, or an ongoing, genocide also can contradict national interests in the sense that democratically elected governments pay much heed to the sentiments and desires of their citizens. This is both a political necessity, in that a government that wishes to be reelected cannot go against public sentiment; and it is a moral and ethical issue, in that government must serve the public interest. When President Clinton's administration refused to call the mass murder in Rwanda genocide, it did so because it knew that such categorization would make it incumbent upon the United States to act, and yet the American public was unwilling to support intervention, especially after the failed American operation in Somalia. Similarly, the United States was unable to intervene in the genocide in Cambodia because domestic public opinion was resolutely opposed to any involvement in Southeast Asia following the Vietnam War.

5. IT MUST ALSO BE NOTED THAT ESPECIALLY IN DEMOCRACIES, those citizens most likely to identify and condemn genocide are also those most suspicious of military intervention in the affairs of other states. Military actions often cause casualties among innocent bystanders and frequently fail to harm the

actual perpetrators. Yet genocide must sometimes be stopped by the force of arms. Conversely, it is also true that some nations may try to implement their own policies of expansion and occupation by claiming to be acting in the name of humanitarian interests. Nevertheless, as we have seen time and again in the past, genocidal regimes rarely respond to negotiations and often must be physically destroyed in order to put an end to their crimes.

Intervention in genocide is therefore in a real sense a test both for the international community and for the nature of politics in democratic states. Citizens cannot expect their governments to do the right thing, but must demonstrate that it is in their interest—and therefore in the national interest—that genocide be prevented, stopped, or punished. States cannot rely on the international community to do the right thing either, but must repeatedly insist that it is in the interest of civilization as a whole to curb crimes against humanity, and that particular national interests will ultimately be served by mobilizing against inhumanity. This challenge refocuses the question of individual responsibility, for only individuals can compel their representatives to engage in international affairs and to adopt international norms and treaties. In this sense, individuals such as Lemkin matter a great deal. In fact, his unique contribution—giving moral outrage a concrete legal form—provided a powerful tool with which individuals, groups, and nations can hold governments and their leaders accountable for the intentional and organized murder of innocents.

1899, 1907	The Hague Conventions, one of the first attempts to create a body of international laws to regulate war
1900	Lemkin born in Wolkowysk (in an area then known as Lithuania)
1915–18	During World War I, over one million Armenians are killed by the Ottoman (Turkish) government; Mehmad Talaat and others live freely in exile after ordering the deaths of innocent civilians
1921	Soghomon Tehlirian kills Mehmed Talaat on the streets of Berlin; Tehlirian is acquitted Lemkin enters law school
1933	Lemkin's paper urges international leaders at the Madrid Conference to make a law against the destruction of religious or ethnic groups which he calls crimes of "vandalism" and "acts of barbarism" Hitler comes to power in Germany
1939–45	World War II and the Nazi Holocaust in Europe
1941	Lemkin escapes Nazi persecution in Poland, immigrates to the United States Winston Churchill refers to the Nazi extermination of Jews, gypsies, and others as "a crime without a name"
1944	Lemkin publishes *Axis Rule in Occupied Europe* in which he coins the word genocide
1945	International Military Tribunal in Nuremberg, Germany is established and marks the first time national leaders are brought to justice by the international community The word genocide is used during the trials to describe Nazi acts against Jews and gypsies The United Nations is founded
1948	Convention on the Prevention and Punishment of the Crime of Genocide and the Declaration of Human Rights are adopted by the United Nations on two consecutive days

1951	The Genocide Convention is ratified at the United Nations
	Lemkin lobbies unsuccessfully to have the United States ratify the treaty
1959	Lemkin dies in New York
1967–86	Senator Proxmire gives daily speeches on the floor of the United States Senate urging members of Congress to ratify the Genocide Convention
1975–79	Cambodian Genocide, approximately 1.7 million Cambodians die
1988	The United States ratifies the Genocide Convention
1991–95	Genocide in the former Yugoslavia
1993	International Criminal Tribunal for the former Yugoslavia is established to prosecute crimes of war and genocide
1994	Rwandan Genocide over 100 days; International Criminal Tribunal for Rwanda is established
1998	Jean-Paul Akayesu, a Rwandan who oversaw some killings of Tutsis, is found guilty of genocide, marking the first conviction for the crime of genocide in an international court
2002	The International Criminal Court is established as a permanent court that tries people accused of genocide, crimes against humanity, and war crimes
2003	Janjaweed militia (supported by the Sudanese government) begins murdering and raping civilians in Darfur
2004	American Secretary of State Colin Powell refers to killings in Darfur as genocide; the first time the United States refers to an ongoing crisis as genocide
	Juan Méndez (a former political prisoner in Argentina) is appointed to become the first United Nations special adviser on the prevention of genocide

OVERVIEW

Born in 1900, Raphael Lemkin devoted most of his life to a single goal: making the world understand and recognize a crime so horrific that there was not even a word for it. Lemkin took a step toward his goal in 1944 when he coined the word "genocide" which means the destruction of a nation or an ethnic group. He said he had created the word by combining the ancient Greek word *genos* (race, tribe) and the Latin *cide* (killing). In 1948, three years after the concentration camps of World War II had been closed forever, the newly formed United Nations used this new word in a treaty that was intended to prevent any future genocides.

Lemkin died a decade later. He had lived long enough to see his word widely accepted and also to see the United Nations treaty, called the Convention on the Prevention and Punishment of the Crime of Genocide, adopted by many nations. But, sadly, recent history reminds us that laws and treaties are not enough to prevent genocide.

KEY QUESTIONS

1. What is genocide? What are the strengths and limitations of the law in preventing genocide and massive human rights violations?

2. How can new words change the way people think about a problem? Can they change people's attitudes?

3. What is sovereignty? Why does it sometimes stand in the way of stopping mass violence?

4. What is the difference between national and international crimes? When do individuals, groups, and nations have the right or duty to intervene on behalf of victims in other countries?

5. What legacy did Lemkin leave for the struggle against state-sponsored violence? What work remains to be done?

"Sovereignty cannot be conceived as the right to kill millions"

They were a respected couple. The man, known as Said Ali Bey, was dignified, highly educated, and thought to be very rich; his wife was an attractive, modern Muslim woman with refined tastes and an independent mind.[1] They were Turkish and had come to Berlin three years earlier, at the end of World War I. Their neighbors often saw them strolling together after dinner.

Credit: Henry Morgenthau

Mehmed Talaat, the Ottoman minister of the interior, was responsible for planning and implementing the Armenian Genocide.

On the evening of March 15, 1921, they were walking in the elegant Charlottenburg district when a young Armenian man came up to Bey and tapped him on the shoulder. He then drew a revolver and shot both of them, hitting Bey in the head, killing him at once and wounding his wife. Passersby who had seen the murder immediately seized the young man and came close to lynching him on the spot.[2] When the police arrived, the assassin pointed at the man he had shot and declared, "It is not I who am the murderer. It is he!"[3]

Soon the whole world learned what this puzzling statement meant and who the two men were. The young Armenian, Soghomon Tehlirian, said the man he had killed was not Said Ali Bey. His real name was Mehmed Talaat, and he had been the minister of the interior of the Ottoman Empire (now Turkey). During World War I, Talaat, who was known as the "Big Boss," had conducted a ruthless campaign against the Armenian people, a Christian minority in the empire. At his trial, Tehlirian described the events he had seen in his own town:

> In 1915 the Armenian populace of Erzerum was suddenly alarmed by the news that the Turkish Government planned violent measures. Shortly afterward the populace was herded together and driven off in columns under the conduct of Turkish soldiers. After being robbed of their money and belongings[,] the massacre, in which my family were victims, took place. After I had seen my brother's skull split, I was hit on the head and lay unconscious probably [for] one or two days.[4]

Evidence presented at Tehlirian's trial showed that in 1915 alone, Talaat had "presided over the killing by firing squad, bayoneting, bludgeoning, and starvation of nearly 1 million Armenians."[5] The plans had been methodically drawn up and carried out. First the Armenian leadership was murdered. Then Armenian men of military age were driven from their villages and either immediately executed or sent to death camps. Then the children, women, and old men were evicted from their homes and forced to make death marches, during which special units attacked them, butchering tens of thousands of people. Those who survived the rapes, the beatings, the murderous attacks, and the hardships of the marches were sent to the desert to die of thirst and hunger.[6]

Germany had been an ally of the Ottoman Empire in World War I. During Tehlirian's trial, it was also revealed that despite the terrible crimes committed by Talaat and his subordinates, the German government had sheltered him and other Ottoman leaders after the war. In Germany, they had enjoyed the comfortable and respectable lives of retired state officials.[7]

Raphael Lemkin, a young Polish Jew who had recently begun studying at the University of Lvov, read about Tehlirian's trial in the newspaper. Horrified, he talked with one of his professors about the case. He asked whether Tehlirian had tried to have Talaat arrested for the massacre of the Armenians before deciding to shoot him himself.

His professor shook his head and stated the awful truth about the lack of international laws to try perpetrators of state-sanctioned crimes: "There was no law under which he [Talaat] could be arrested. . . . Consider the case of a farmer who owns a flock of chickens. He kills them, and this is his business. If you

Soghomon Tehlirian, an Armenian survivor of the genocide, killed Talaat on the street in Berlin and was later acquitted.

Credit: Project SAVE Armenian Photograph Archives, Inc., Courtesy of Faith Cass

interfere, you are trespassing."

Lemkin was shocked. "But the Armenians are not chickens. Certainly—"

The professor coolly went on, "You cannot interfere with the internal affairs of a nation without infringing on that nation's sovereignty."

To Lemkin, this did not make sense. "It is a crime for Tehlirian to kill a man, but it is not a crime for his oppressor to kill more than a million men. This is most inconsistent."[8] But Lemkin's professor simply stated facts: After World War I, when the victorious states sought to charge Turkey and Germany for crimes they committed against their own citizens, they had no law on which to rely. While war crimes were already defined by the international community, no agreement on crimes such as the ones the Ottoman Empire perpetrated against its Armenian citizens was in existence.[9]

Tehlirian was eventually acquitted on the grounds of temporary insanity, but Lemkin remained haunted by the case. How could the world ignore the fact that known murderers were living happily in democratic nations? Lemkin began to study the background of the Talaat case. He learned that after World War I, a Turkish court had actually found Talaat and other Ottoman leaders guilty of mass murder and had sentenced them to death. But he also discovered that many of these condemned officials, including Talaat, had fled before their sentences could be carried out; the others had been released.[10] Was it really possible that nearly everyone responsible for one of the greatest massacres in history had escaped without any consequences?

The more he learned about the Armenian massacre and what had happened after it, the more outraged Lemkin felt. He could not accept the idea that a man could be punished if he killed another man, but a man who had killed millions could not be prosecuted for this crime. In his autobiography, Lemkin asked, "Why was killing a million people a less serious crime than killing a single individual?"[11] The two things were completely contradictory.

It seemed clear to Lemkin that the ideal of sovereignty described by his professor—a nation's right to determine what happens to its citizens and within its borders—should not be used as a shield for nations that persecuted and murdered their own people. He thought that sovereignty should be redefined to mean all the things a nation does for the benefit of its own people—such things as conducting relationships with other countries as well as internal activities like building schools and roads. But, he said, "Sovereignty cannot be conceived as the right to kill millions of innocent people."[12]

To cure the illness of a world where men like Talaat went free, strong medicine was needed. Lemkin soon came to believe that the cure for mass murder and gross abuses of human rights would have to come through international law. But he discovered that very few international laws existed to deal with such crises. In addition, no international court had jurisdiction over crimes committed within a sovereign nation's borders. This seemed wrong to Lemkin, and he began to think about how it could be changed.

CONNECTIONS

1. The answer Lemkin received from his professor reflected the state of international law in the beginning of the twentieth century: back then there were no laws that gave states authority to intervene in the internal affairs of other nations. To do so would undermine the idea of sovereignty, that is, the right of every nation to conduct its internal affairs independently. What limits would you set on a nation's sovereignty? When should the international community impose laws on other countries?

2. Lemkin wondered, "Why is the killing of a million a lesser crime than the killing of a single individual?" What can be done to stop nations that turn against their own people?

3. Lemkin was outraged when he heard that the mass murder of the Armenians went unpunished. How could he turn his moral outrage into action? What could he do?

4. Without a court to judge the perpetrators, what options did the Armenians have after the genocide?

FRANCE, GREAT BRITAIN, AND RUSSIA JOINT DECLARATION

In 1915 accounts from international observers, politicians, and reporters alerted the world to the unfolding massacre of the Armenian minority in the Ottoman Empire. Outraged, Russia (who had a significant Armenian minority) called on its French and British allies to join in warning the Ottoman leadership that it would be held accountable for its "fresh crimes . . . against Christianity and civilization." Britain, which was slow to respond at first, countered this proposal by turning to a universal language: It wanted to stay away from language that simply portrayed these unspeakable acts as crimes committed by Muslims against Christians (or simply a violation of Christian values). The British asked that the declaration condemn "crimes against civilization," namely, barbaric acts that violated the principles of the entire civilized world. Lemkin relied upon these distinctions in his Madrid paper (see Reading 2). The Russian foreign minister, Sergei Sazonov, then came up with a compromise and coined the phrase "crimes against humanity and civilization." It was also one of the first times a state was accused of committing a crime against its own citizens.[13]

```
              Department of State, Washington
                    May 29, 1915

Amembassy [American Embassy],
Constantinople
French Foreign Office requests following notice be given
Turkish Government.

May 24th

   For about a month the Kurd and Turkish population of
Armenia has been massacring Armenians with the connivance
and often assistance of Ottoman authorities. Such massacres
took place in middle April at Erzerum, Dertchun, Eguine,
Akn, Bitlis, Mush, Sassun, Zeitun, and throughout Cilicia.
Inhabitants of about one hundred villages near Van were all
murdered. In that city [the] Armenian quarter is besieged by
Kurds. At the same time in Constantinople Ottoman Government
ill-treats inoffensive Armenian population. In view of those
new crimes of Turkey against humanity and civilization, the
Allied governments announce publicly to the Sublime-Porte
that they will hold personally responsible [for] these crimes
all members of the Ottoman government and those of their
agents who are implicated in such massacres.[14]
```

TELEGRAM SENT CIPHER

Department of State,

Washington, May 29, 1915.

Amembassy,

Constantinople.

715 French Foreign Office requests following notice be given Turkish Government. Quote. May 24th. For about a month the Kurd and Turkish population of Armenia has been massacring Armenians with the connivance and often assistance of Ottoman authorities. Such massacres took place in middle April (?) at Erzerum, Dertohun, Eguine, Akn, Bitlis, Moush, Sassoun, Zeitoun, and through Cilicia. Inhabitants of about one hundred villages near Van were all murdered. In that city Armenian quarter is besieged by Kurds. At the same time in Constantinople government ill treats inoffensive Armenian population. In view of these new crimes of Turkey against humanity and civilization the Allied governments announce publicly to the Sublime Porte that they will hold personally responsible these crimes all members of the Ottoman government and those of their agents who are implicated in such massacres. Unquote.

Communicate in Paraphrase

867.4016/67

3 P/P1

Enciphered by

Sent by operator AO May 29 1915 OK 9 A

The telegram sent from the American embassy to the Turkish (Ottoman) government

BEYOND THE READING

Details about the Armenian Genocide and the trials held in Turkey after World War I can be found in the Facing History and Ourselves resource book *Crimes Against Humanity and Civilization: The Genocide of the Armenians* (Brookline: Facing History and Ourselves, 2004).

For information about the Ottoman government's actions during and after the Armenian Genocide, see Andrew Goldberg, *The Armenian Genocide*, VHS (New York: Two Cats Production, 2005). The film, which includes a rare interview with Raphael Lemkin, also explores the Turkish denial of the genocide.

To see how another country has dealt with the process of seeking justice in the wake of mass violence, download the Facing History resource book *Facing the Truth* (www.facinghistory.org/facingthetruth), which examines the difficult choices made by South Africans in the aftermath of apartheid.

For a broader survey that compares the strategies used in Rwanda, Germany, Northern Ireland, and South Africa to foster justice and reconciliation in the aftermath of mass violence, please visit Facing History's interactive module *Transitional Justice: Repairing Self and Society* (www.facinghistory.org/tjmodule).

1 "Talaat is Mourned as Germany's Friend," *New York Times*, March 18, 1921.

2 "Talaat Pasha Slain in Berlin Suburb," *New York Times*, March 16, 1921.

3 "Assassin Boasts of Talaat's Death," *New York Times*, March 17, 1921.

4 "Says Mother's Ghost Ordered Him to Kill," *New York Times*, June 3, 1921.

5 Samantha Power, *"A Problem from Hell": America and the Age of Genocide* (New York: Basic Books, 2002), 1.

6 Details about the Armenian Genocide can be found in Facing History's resource book entitled *Crimes Against Humanity and Civilization: The Genocide of the Armenians* (Brookline: Facing History and Ourselves, 2004).

7 J. Michael Hagopian's documentary *Germany and the Secret Genocide*, VHS (Thousand Oaks: Armenian Film Foundation, 2003) discusses the involvement of Germany (Turkey's wartime ally) in the Armenian Genocide. The film is available at the Facing History Lending Library.

8 Robert Merrill Bartlett, *They Stand Invincible: Men Who Are Reshaping Our World* (New York: Thomas Y. Crowell Company, 1959), 96-97. The story is also vividly told by Power in *A Problem from Hell*, 17.

9 Taner Akçam, *From Empire to Republic: Turkish Nationalism and the Armenian Genocide* (New York: Zed Books, 2004) 185-90.

10 For details on these trials, see Gary Jonathan Bass, *Stay the Hand of Vengeance: The Politics of War Crimes Tribunals* (Princeton: Princeton University Press, 2000), 106-46. On Lemkin's reaction to the trials, see Steven L. Jacobs, "Raphael Lemkin and the Armenian Genocide," in *Looking Backward, Moving Forward: Confronting the Armenian Genocide*, ed. Richard G. Hovannisian (New Brunswick: Transaction Publishers, 2003), 127.

11 Raphael Lemkin, *Totally Unofficial Man: The Autobiography of Raphael Lemkin*, in *Pioneers of Genocide Studies*, ed. Steven L. Jacobs and Samuel Totten (New Brunswick: Transaction Books, 2002), 371.

12 Ibid.

13 Bass, *Stay the Hand of Vengeance*, 115-17.

14 France, Great Britain and Russia Joint Declaration (May 24, 1915), Armenian National Institute website, http://www.armenian-genocide.org/Affirmation.160/current_category.7/affirmation_detail.html (accessed on October 11, 2006).

Crimes Against Individuals as Members of a Larger Group

Raphael Lemkin was born in 1900 on a farm near the town of Wolkowysk in a part of czarist Russia then known as Lithuania (now part of the Republic of Belarus). He later described it as a land "in which various nationalities lived together for many centuries." The Poles, Russians, and Jews of this area "disliked each other, and even fought each other." But "in spite of these turmoils," Lemkin wrote, they shared a "feeling of common destiny that prevented them from destroying one another completely."[1]

Credit: Tomek Wisniewski; permission granted by BE&W Agencja Fotograficzna Sp.z o.o., Poland

Wolkowysk circa 1911. Raphael Lemkin was born in this part of Lithuania, where people of different groups lived together for centuries.

Lemkin recalled a peaceful childhood: "The children. . . spent their days together in one happy gang."[2] Poems and folk tales shared by the fireside fed their imaginations; stories of innocence and injustice, of the suffering of the poor, and of "people bow[ing] to false gods. . .

the gods of greed and power" fostered Lemkin's awareness of human misery. Yet the same songs that lamented humankind's oppression of other humans also offered "hope for a betterment of the world, for the cessation of evil, for the protection of the weak."[3]

Lemkin's interest in other cultures led him to study foreign languages. He soon mastered Polish, German, Russian, French, Italian, Hebrew, and Yiddish, and then he turned to philology—the study of the evolution of language itself. But the massacre of the Armenians in the Ottoman Empire during World War I changed his mind (see Reading 1). The fate of the Armenians, and the failure of the victorious Allies to bring Ottoman and German war criminals to justice after the war, appalled Lemkin. In 1921 he enrolled at the University of Lvov in Poland to study international law. (Lvov is now in Ukraine.)[4]

Lemkin learned as much as he could about both ancient and modern law; he wanted to find a way to define the slaughter of national, racial, and religious groups as a crime in legal as well as moral terms. After graduation, he worked briefly as a lawyer but then entered public service; soon he became the deputy public prosecutor of Warsaw, the Polish capital.[5] During the early 1930s, Lemkin spent countless hours thinking about how to create a legal, international safety net for all minorities.

The first opportunity to introduce his ideas (and what would become his lifelong crusade) to the international

A meeting of the League of Nations in Madrid. Lemkin's paper on barbarism and vandalism was presented at the League of Nations in Madrid in 1933.

Credit: York University Clara Thomas Archive & Special Collections, Walter Alexander Riddell fonds, Photographs, 1926-1936, 1970-005/005 (01). ASC Image #1869.

community came in 1933 when the League of Nations met in Madrid to draw up a set of agreements that would define international crimes.[6] The timing proved prophetic: in that same year, the Nazi government enacted antisemitic legislation in Germany and thousands of Jews began to flee the country. Another hint of the Nazis' intentions came when the German delegation marched out of the League of Nations right before the meetings began.[7]

Hoping to please the Nazis, the Polish government ordered Lemkin not to attend the meetings in Madrid. But Lemkin was determined not to be stopped, and he found a delegate who agreed to present his proposal for him. The proposal began with a list of precedents (previous rules and laws) that were based on the idea that some crimes extend beyond national boundaries and destabilize the world community as a whole. These precedents included long-standing laws against piracy, counterfeiting, and the slave trade, as well as newer international laws against the use of "any instrument capable of producing public danger" (this was a ban on what we now call terrorism).[8] Lemkin showed that all of these laws were based on the fact that certain acts were considered crimes by most nations of the world; therefore, a person who committed such an act could be arrested and brought to trial in any country, no matter where the crime had been committed or where the person lived.

Equally important, Lemkin moved beyond showing the historical precedents for international laws and defined a new kind of international crime as:

[Acts] carried out against an *individual as a member of a collectivity*. The goal of the [crime] is not only to harm an individual, but also to cause damage to the collectivity to which the [individual] belongs. Offenses of this type bring harm not only to human rights, but also and most especially they undermine the fundamental basis of the social order.[9]

Lemkin called these crimes "acts of barbarism." They included religious massacres, pogroms (massacres) against Jews and other minority groups, even embargoes on food and medicine; their purpose was to destroy a group identified by a shared ethnicity, religion, or social identity.

Lemkin carried his ideas one step further. He did not want to limit his definition of international crimes to the destruction of human beings; for him, social and cultural life was as important as physical existence. So another element of international crime included the "systematic and organized destruction of the art and cultural heritage in which the unique genius and achievement of a collectivity are revealed in fields of science, art and literature." He called this cultural devastation "vandalism."[10] In an essay written after World War II, Lemkin explained the importance of protecting the cultural achievements of ethnic groups:

Our whole heritage is a product of the contributions of all nations. We can best understand this when we realize how impoverished our culture would be if the peoples doomed by Germany, such

German soldiers on their way to Poland. The inscription on the railway car reads: "We are going to Poland to strike at the Jews." Lemkin was forced to flee when Germany invaded Poland in 1939.

as the Jews, had not been permitted to create the Bible, or to give birth to an Einstein, a Spinoza; if the Poles had not had the opportunity to give to the world a Copernicus, a Chopin, a Curie; the Czechs, a Huss, a Dvorak; the Greeks, a Plato and a Socrates; the Russians, a Tolstoy and a Shostakovich.[11]

Such acts of "vandalism," Lemkin argued, must be the subject of international law because they were committed not simply against a specific group but against civilization as a whole. They undermined the culture we share as human beings.

But Lemkin's ambitious proposal fell on deaf ears in 1933. The delegates to the League of Nations conference brushed it aside, some for political reasons, others because they thought that crimes against humanity happened "too seldom to legislate."[12]

❖   ❖   ❖

Six years later, on September 1, 1939, Nazi soldiers invaded Poland. Before Warsaw was overwhelmed, the Polish government broadcast a warning on the radio: every able-bodied male must leave the country immediately. Lemkin slipped on a coat, put his shaving kit under his arm, and boarded a train. But German bombers destroyed the train, killing hundreds of people. Lemkin and other survivors fled into the nearby woods. His hopes of reaching the safety a colleague had offered him in Sweden began to fade. "The distance appeared to me now insurmountable. I was a man without a tomorrow."[13]

Still determined to escape, Lemkin managed to see his family in Wolkowysk one more time. But he could not convince them to join him in trying to reach the free world. Looking into their eyes, he read a simple message: "Do not talk of our leaving this warm home, our beds, our stores of food, the security of our customs. We will have to suffer but we will survive somehow."[14]

Lemkin wrote later that he could understand his family's decision to stay in their homes: "What did I have to offer them? A nomadic life, a refugee's lot."[15] Forty-nine of his relatives, including his parents, were eventually murdered in the Holocaust, the type of crime he had foreseen decades before.

CONNECTIONS

1. Lemkin wrote of a "common destiny" that kept the Poles, Russians, and Jews who lived in the villages and towns near Lvov from destroying each other. What do you think Lemkin meant by the phrase "common sense of destiny?" What encourages a sense of common destiny between different nationalities? What actions can destroy it?

2. Lemkin believed that some crimes harm the world community as a whole. What crimes fall under that category? In what ways do these crimes transcend, or go beyond, national boundaries?

3. Why did Lemkin distinguish between crimes of vandalism and crimes of barbarism? What point was he making?

4. Genocide scholar Israel Charny identified 10 processes that indicate the coming of genocide. Among the warning signs he mentioned are the decline in the value of human life, excessive appreciation for and use of state power (even when it abuses its citizens), the exercise of violence and destructiveness in everyday life, and the dehumanization of minorities (the depiction of a group as less than human, which means that it's okay to hurt its members).[16] Come up with your own list of indications that one group may be intent on destroying another.

LEMKIN'S MADRID PAPER (1933)

In 1933 the League of Nations met in Madrid to define a new list of international crimes. This was Lemkin's first opportunity to introduce his thoughts about the need to outlaw mass murder to the international community.[17] But the Polish government, which hoped to please the Nazis, ordered Lemkin not to attend the meetings. Lemkin did not give up. He found a delegate who agreed to present his proposal for him. The text below includes excerpts from this proposal.

Drawing on a handful of existing international laws, Lemkin argued that international laws were based on the idea that certain acts were considered so dangerous to the international community that most nations of the world viewed them as crimes. A person who committed such an act could therefore be arrested and brought to trial in any country, no matter where the crime had been committed or where the person lived. This proposal was based on the principle of "universal jurisdiction," or in Lemkin's terms, "the principle of universal repression." Lemkin argued that attempts to destroy minority groups were examples of such international crimes. Lemkin suggested a broad definition for the crime: both the murder of minority group members ("acts of barbarism"), and the destruction of a group's cultural heritage ("acts of vandalism") would be subject to international prohibition. He felt that protecting cultural heritage was essential because he believed that the legacy of all human groups ("collectivities"), contribute to an ever-expanding universal, human culture.[18]

THE CONCEPT of offenses against the law of nations . . . comes from the interdependent struggle of the civilized world community against criminality. From the formal point of view, this solidarity appears in the principle of universal repression [or universal jurisdiction], based upon the principle that an offender can be brought to justice in the place where he is apprehended. . . independently of where the crime was committed and the nationality of the author. . . . This is because such a perpetrator is regarded as the enemy of the whole international community and in all States he will be pursued for crimes universally harmful to all the international community.

The principle of universal repression does not apply to all crimes, but only those considered so particularly dangerous as to present a threat to the interests, either of a material nature or of a moral nature, of the entire international community (offenses against the law of nations). That offenses in this category are universally prohibited attests to the fact that there is a legal conscience of the civilized international community. . . .

THE ACTS OF BARBARITY

IF WE ANALYZE THE DRIVING IDEAS of certain offenses against the law of nations, like trade in slaves and trade in women and children, we see that if these offenses are regarded as punishable, it is due to humane principles. In these cases the principles are, above all, to protect the freedom and the dignity of the individual, and to prevent human beings from being treated as merchandise.

Some other provisions [or legal measures] relating to the offenses against the law of nations relate to the protection and maintenance of the normal peaceful relations between collectivities [or groups], for example the offense of the propaganda for a war of aggression. The prohibitions of such attacks have as a goal to assure good cultural and economic relations between nations. . . .

However, there are offenses which combine these two elements [of maintaining peaceful relations between nations and protecting the freedom and the dignity of the individual]. In particular these are attacks carried out against an individual as a member of a collectivity [or a group]. The goal of the author [of the crime] is not only to harm an individual, but, also to cause damage to the collectivity to which the latter belongs. Offenses of this type bring harm not only to human rights, but also and most especially they undermine the fundamental basis of the social order.

LET US CONSIDER, first and foremost, acts of extermination directed against the ethnic, religious or social collectivities whatever the motive (political, religious, etc.); for example massacres, pogroms, actions undertaken to ruin the economic existence of the members of a collectivity, etc. Also belonging in this category are all sorts of brutalities which attack the dignity of the individual in cases where these acts of humiliation have their source in a campaign of extermination directed against the collectivity in which the victim is a member.

Taken as a whole, all the acts of this character constitute an offense against the law of nations which we will call by the name "barbarity." Taken separately all these acts are punishable in the respective codes; considered together, however, they should constitute offenses against the law of nations [or international law] by reason of their common feature which is to endanger both the existence of the collectivity concerned and the entire social order.

The impact of acts like these usually exceed relations between individuals. They shake the very basis of harmony in social relations between particular collectivities. . . .

ACTS OF VANDALISM
(Destruction of the culture and works of art)

AN ATTACK TARGETING A COLLECTIVITY can also take the form of systematic and organized destruction of the art and cultural heritage in which the unique genius and achievement of a collectivity are revealed in fields of science, arts and literature. The contribution of any particular collectivity to world culture as a whole, forms the wealth of all of humanity, even while exhibiting unique characteristics.

Thus, the destruction of a work of art of any nation must be regarded as acts of vandalism directed against world culture [or civilization]. The author [of the crime] causes not only the immediate irrevocable losses of the destroyed work as property and as the culture of the collectivity directly concerned (whose unique genius contributed to the creation of this work); it is also all humanity which experiences a loss by this act of vandalism.

In the acts of barbarity, as well as in those of vandalism, the asocial and destructive spirit of the author is made evident. This spirit, by definition, is the opposite of the culture and progress of humanity. It throws the evolution of ideas back to the bleak period of the Middle Ages. Such acts shock the conscience of all humanity, while generating extreme anxiety about the future. For all these reasons, acts of vandalism and barbarity must be regarded as offenses against the law of nations.[19]

1 Raphael Lemkin, *Totally Unofficial Man: The Autobiography of Raphael Lemkin, in Pioneers of Genocide Studies*, ed. Steven L. Jacobs and Samuel Totten (New Brunswick: Transaction Books, 2002), 368.

2 Ibid., 369.

3 Ibid., 370.

4 Samantha Power, *"A Problem from Hell": America and the Age of Genocide* (New York: Basic Books, 2002), 21.

5 Robert Merrill Bartlett, *They Stand Invincible: Men Who Are Reshaping Our World* (New York: Thomas Y. Crowell Company, 1959), 97.

6 For Lemkin's contribution to this discussion, see Daniel Marc Segesser and Myriam Gesser, "Raphael Lemkin and the International Debate on the Punishment of War Crimes (1919-1948)," *Journal of Genocide Research* 7 (December 2005), 457.

7 The League of Nations was formed after World War I to promote international cooperation, peace, and security as part of the Treaty of Versailles—the peace settlement signed at the end of this war. Despite President Woodrow Wilson's leadership in forming the League, the United States Congress refused to ratify the Treaty of Versailles and make the United States a partner of the League. With no military support, the League of Nations was ineffective in preventing the military aggression that led to World War II. In October 1945, the responsibilities of the League of Nations were signed over to the United Nations.

8 Raphael Lemkin, "Acts Constituting a General (Transitional) Danger Considered as Offense against the Law of Nations," Prevent Genocide International website, http://www.preventgenocide.org/lemkin/madrid1933-english. htm#1 (accessed on October 10, 2005). Prevent Genocide International is a nonprofit educational organization established in 1998 and dedicated to eliminating the crime of genocide.

9 Ibid. Emphasis added.

10 Ibid.

11 Raphael Lemkin, "Genocide," *American Scholar* 15 (1946), 228. This article may also be viewed at the Prevent Genocide website, www.preventgenocide.org/lemkin/americanscholar1946.htm (accessed September 26, 2005).

12 Power, *A Problem from Hell*, 22.

13 Lemkin, *Totally Unofficial Man*, 374.

14 Ibid., 375

15 Ibid.

16 Israel W. Charny (ed.), "Genocide Early Warning System," *Encyclopedia of Genocide* (Santa Barbara: ABC-Clio, 1999), 257-60.

17 For Lemkin's contribution to this discussion, see Daniel Marc Segesser and Myriam Gesser, "Raphael Lemkin and the International Debate on the Punishment of War Crimes," (1919-1948), 457.

18 Raphael Lemkin, "Acts Constituting a General (Transitional) Danger Considered as Offense against the Law of Nations," October 1933, Prevent Genocide International website, http://www.preventgenocide.org/lemkin/madrid1933-english.htm#1 (accessed on October 10, 2005). Prevent Genocide International is a nonprofit educational organization established in 1998 and dedicated to eliminating the crime of genocide.

19 Ibid.

"A crime without a name"

In spring 1941, after a journey of 14,000 miles, Lemkin arrived at Duke University in North Carolina, where he had been hired to teach international law. But his mind was on more urgent matters: Europe was burning and time was running out. Night and day Lemkin struggled to figure out how to persuade America to join the Allies and to help rescue Europe's minorities. One day he received a brief message from his parents; they had received the news of his safe arrival in North Carolina and they wished him well.

"Something within myself told me that in this letter they were saying goodbye," Lemkin recalled. Within the next three years, almost every one of the 20,000 Jews who lived in Wolkowysk was killed in Nazi gas chambers.[1]

A few months later, on August 24, 1941, Prime Minister Winston Churchill addressed the people of Great Britain in a radio broadcast. He spoke of the "barbaric fury" of the German troops who were savaging Europe. The Nazis, he said, had linked "the most deadly instruments of war-science . . . to the extreme refinements of treachery and the most brutal exhibitions of ruthlessness." He told his listeners that

whole districts are being exterminated. Scores of thousands—literally scores of thousands—of executions in cold blood are being perpetrated by the German police troops upon the Russian patriots who defend their native soil. Since the Mongol invasions of Europe in the sixteenth century, there has never been methodical, merciless butchery on such a scale, or approaching such a scale.[2]

Churchill's final words were dramatic: "We are in the presence of a crime without a name."[3]

Churchill's statement made Lemkin change his approach: rather than trying to persuade America to enter the war, he would write a book to describe how the Nazis were using law to justify their systematic destruction of the Jews and other European minorities. "My nights turned into nightmares," Lemkin wrote in his autobiography. "In the midst of the turmoil, I was writing feverishly."[4]

From Duke, Lemkin moved to Washington, DC, where he worked for the Board of Economic Warfare; then, in 1944, the Department of War recruited him as an expert on international law. By this time, most European and American policy makers had heard of the camps where so many of Europe's Jews had been murdered. "All over Europe," Lemkin wrote, "the Nazis were writing the book of death with the blood of my brethren."[5] But in Washington,

> **"We are in the presence of a crime without a name."**

very few paid attention. Lemkin and a handful of others felt that they were witnessing a conspiracy of silence.[6]

In 1944 the Carnegie Endowment for International Peace published Lemkin's *Axis Rule in Occupied Europe*, the monumental book he had been working on with such dedication. In addition to describing the fate of Europe's occupied nations, it had grown to include a comprehensive list of the decrees and laws issued by the Nazis in order to conquer and destroy these nations; Lemkin wanted to show how the Nazis were using laws to undermine civil rights and legitimize mass murder.

A small section of the 721-page book discussed terminology, which Lemkin had been thinking about long before Churchill's speech about the "crime without a name." In choosing to coin a new word for murderous violence directed at a specific group, Lemkin had rejected a number of existing possibilities, including the term "race murder," which Henry Morgenthau, Sr., the United States' ambassador to the Ottoman Empire, used in his reports on the massacres of Armenians in 1915 (see Reading 1).[7]

Alternatively, Lemkin could have adopted the term "crimes against

humanity" which the Allies used in charging the Ottoman leadership for its role in these crimes. This phrase emerged out of a growing interest in the universal rights of individuals that reflected the increase in the political power of the people (and the corresponding erosion in the absolute power of monarchs and emperors) in eighteenth-century Europe and America.[8] During the nineteenth century, people began to refer to actions designed to protect these rights as "humanitarian" (which means a concern for all humans

Armenian survivors hold a burial service for the victims of the Armenian Genocide. In 1915 the Allies declared the massacres of the Armenians a crime against humanity.

or humanity). Behind these humanitarian concerns was the idea that some crimes are so horrific that they violate not only the laws protecting individuals of a specific country but also the basic principles we share as human beings.

Nineteenth-century humanitarian efforts

to protect civilians in times of war grew out of these sentiments.[9] References to the protection of civilians in times of war were made in several international treaties. These treaties also served as the first building blocks of the emerging international law and were codified in the Hague Conventions of 1899 and 1907, which set rules and regulations for the humane treatment of civilians during war.[10]

Despite the important moral implications of the phrase "crimes against humanity," Lemkin found it both imprecise and narrow: the association of the term with warfare excluded the mass murder of groups of people when no war was conducted—that was the case of the crimes committed against the Jews and other minorities in Germany before the beginning of World War II in 1939. On the other hand, the term was too broad: mass killing of members of a specific group constituted but one of many forms of the offenses included in the definitions of crimes against humanity.[11]

None of these terms captured the systematic nature and brutality of the crimes against the Jews and the Armenians; they also did not suggest the careful and cold-blooded planning that had led up to these crimes or the targeting of members of a specific ethnic group. And the words "barbarism" and "vandalism," which Lemkin

had used a decade earlier in his proposal to the League of Nations conference (see Reading 2), failed to catch the public's imagination and did not become widely used.

What kind of word was needed? It had to mean the murder of a particular group, but it also had to include depriving such a group of civil rights and excluding them from many ordinary aspects of life (such as certain kinds of jobs or opportunities for education). In a draft of an unpublished article entitled "The New Word and the New Idea," Lemkin wrote that "new words are always created when a social phenomenon strikes at our consciousness with great force." Some words are created unintentionally in the course of human history; others are coined deliberately in an effort to clarify and direct public attention to emerging social problems. Lemkin saw words as humanity's way of responding to the changing social reality. For him, language was not just the "means of communication between man and mankind" but an "index of civilization," a "social testimony" to humanity's moral achievements, beliefs, and even aspirations.[12]

Lemkin finally settled on genocide, a word that he invented and defined as "the destruction of a nation or an ethnic group." It was compounded, he said,

> **Lemkin finally settled on genocide, a word that he invented and defined as "the destruction of a nation or an ethnic group."**

"from the ancient Greek word *genos* (race, tribe) and the Latin *cide* (killing), thus corresponding in its formation to such words as tyrannicide, homicide, infanticide, etc." To distinguish genocide from mass murder, Lemkin argued that "genocide does not necessarily mean the immediate destruction of a nation." [13] Nor did it have to involve the use of weapons or direct physical force. Genocide would

> signify a coordinated plan of different actions aiming at the destruction of essential foundations of the life of national groups, with the aim of annihilating the groups themselves. The objectives of such a plan would be disintegration of the political and social institutions, of culture, language, national feelings, religion, and economic existence of national groups, and the destruction of the personal security, liberty, health, dignity, and even the lives of the individuals belonging to such groups.[14]

In conclusion, Lemkin said that "Genocide is directed against the national group as an entity, and the actions involved are directed against individuals, not in their individual capacity, but as members of the national group."[15] This was an important element of the definition of genocide: people were killed or excluded not because of anything they did or said or thought but simply because they were members of a particular group. For Lemkin, genocide was an international crime: a threat to international peace, to humanity's shared beliefs, to the universal human civilization that included every group's contributions.[16]

Lemkin's new word caught on quickly, and soon it became part of everyday language. Early in 1950 it made its first appearance in the Merriam-Webster company's authoritative English dictionary.[17] The intentional destruction of human groups was no longer a crime without a name.

Lemkin believed that the next step should be the formal outlawing of genocide. Before this could happen, the world needed a legal framework that would not only label genocide as a crime but also explain how it would be stopped and how those who committed genocide would be punished. Lemkin pointed out that human beings are unique: they make laws to live by—which distinguishes them from all other beings—and they are also able to change their laws to reflect their common interests (laws, Lemkin argued, are like language: you can make new laws in the same way that you make new words). In Lemkin's words, "Only man has law. Law must be built."[18] And to ensure that this building process leads to good and not evil, Lemkin said that law "must have a social and human meaning. . . . Legal technicalities and niceties in international law have been and must continue to be subordinate to the basic principles of human conscience and responsibility." He concluded, "International law should be an instrument for human progress and justice."[19]

CONNECTIONS

1. Numerous words that described mass killings were available to Lemkin—crimes against humanity, slaughter, race murder, and holocaust (as well as their equivalents in other languages). He rejected all of them in favor of a word he made up himself. Does the word genocide convey something the other terms do not? Why did Lemkin think that inventing new words was an important element in the campaign to outlaw crimes like genocide?

2. Lemkin believed that new words are created when new social phenomena "strike at our consciousness." How can finding the right words help us understand new problems? What is the role of language in dealing with social ills? How do innovations in language educate those who use the language?

3. The Nazis used law to make their discriminatory policies against the Jews and other European minorities acceptable. Lemkin thought that this was an illegitimate use of the law and that laws "must continue to be subordinated to the basic principles of human conscience and responsibilities." What did he mean when he said this? Are there universal moral principles that we should uphold? Do you agree with Lemkin's position that the law is "an instrument for human progress?" Can you think of times when law has been, as Lemkin argues, "an instrument for human progress?" Are there examples of laws that have not been instruments for human progress?

PRIME MINISTER WINSTON CHURCHILL'S BROADCAST TO THE WORLD ABOUT THE MEETING WITH PRESIDENT ROOSEVELT

The scope of World War II increased dramatically in 1941, as Nazi forces and their Axis allies pushed eastward towards the borders of the Soviet Union. On their way to Moscow, the Nazis and their allies inflicted unprecedented destruction, razing thousands of villages and towns and murdering hundreds of thousands of both soldiers and civilians. When news about the barbaric nature of the German offensive reached England, Prime Minister Winston Churchill arranged for talks with President Franklin D. Roosevelt and his advisors in mid-sea. On his return to England, he made the speech below. Lemkin later claimed that this radio address focused his attention on the urgent need to find a word to describe the kind of crime the German troops committed in Europe.

British Prime Minister Winston Churchill warned others about the barbaric fury of the Nazis. In 1941, he called it a "crime without a name."

August 24, 1941

I thought you would like me to tell you something about the voyage which I made across the ocean to meet our great friend, the President [Franklin D. Roosevelt] of the United States. Exactly where we met is a secret, but I don't think I shall be indiscreet if I go so far as to say that it was somewhere in the Atlantic.

In a spacious, land-locked bay which reminded me of the west coast of Scotland, powerful American warships, protected by strong flotillas and far-ranging aircraft, awaited our arrival and, as it were, stretched out a hand to help us in. . . .

This was a meeting which marks forever in the pages of history the taking up by the English-speaking nations, amid all this peril, tumult and confusion, of the guidance of the fortunes of the broad toiling masses in all the continents, and our loyal effort, without any clog of selfish interest, to lead them forward out of the miseries into which they have been plunged, back to the broad high road of freedom and justice. This is the highest honour and the most glorious opportunity which could ever have come to any branch of the human race.

When one beholds how many currents of extraordinary and terrible events have flowed together to make this harmony, even the most skeptical person must have the feeling that we all have the chance to play our part and do our duty in some great design, the end of which no mortal can foresee. Awful and horrible things are happening in these days.

The whole of Europe has been wrecked and trampled down by the mechanical weapons and barbaric fury of the Nazis. The most deadly instruments of war science have been joined to the extreme refinements of treachery and the most brutal exhibitions of ruthlessness and thus have formed a combine of aggression, the like of which has never been known, before which the rights, the traditions, the characteristics and the structure of many ancient, honoured States and peoples have been laid prostrate and are now ground down under the heel and terror of a monster.

The Austrians, the Czechs, the Poles, the Norwegians, the Danes, the Belgians, the Dutch, the Greeks, the Croats and the Serbs, above all the great French nation, have been stunned and pinioned. Italy, Hungary, Rumania, Bulgaria have bought a shameful respite by becoming the jackals of the tiger. But their situation is very little different and will presently be indistinguishable from that of his victims. Sweden, Spain and Turkey stand appalled, wondering which will be struck down next. Here then is the vast pit into which all the most famous States and races of Europe have been flung and from which, unaided, they can never climb.

But all this did not satiate Adolf Hitler. He made a treaty of non-aggression with Russia [Soviet Union], just as he made one with Turkey, in order to keep them quiet until he was ready to attack them. And then, nine weeks ago today, without a vestige of provocation, he hurled millions of soldiers with all their apparatus upon the neighbor he had called his friend with the avowed object of destroying Russia and tearing her in pieces. . . .

Ah, but this time it was not so easy. This time it was not all one way. The Russian Armies and all the peoples of the Russian Republic have rallied to the defence of their hearths and homes. For the first time Nazi blood has flowed in a fearful torrent. Certainly a million and a half, perhaps two million of Nazi cannon-fodder, have bitten the dust of the endless plains of Russia. The tremendous battle rages along nearly two thousand miles of front. The Russians fight with magnificent devotion. Not only that, our generals who have visited the Russian front line report with admiration the efficiency of their military organization and the excellence of their equipment. The aggressor is surprised, startled, staggered. For the first time in his experience mass murder has become unprofitable. He retaliates by the most frightful cruelties. As his armies advance, whole districts are being exterminated. Scores of thousands, literally scores of thousands of executions in cold blood are being perpetrated by the German police troops upon the Russian patriots who defend their native soil. Since the Mongol invasions of Europe in the sixteenth century there has never been methodical, merciless butchery on such a scale or approaching such a scale. And this is but the beginning. Famine and pestilence have yet to follow in the bloody ruts of Hitler's tanks.

We are in the presence of a crime without a name.[20]

GENOCIDE — A NEW TERM AND NEW CONCEPTION FOR DESTRUCTION OF NATIONS

In 1944 the Carnegie Endowment for International Peace published Lemkin's *Axis Rule in Occupied Europe*, the book he had written during War World II. The monumental work not only described the fate of Europe's occupied nations, it also provided a comprehensive list of the decrees and laws that the Nazis had issued in order to conquer and destroy these nations. Lemkin included this list because he wanted to show how the Nazis used laws to undermine civil rights and legitimize the massive murder of several occupied minorities. A small section of the 721-page book discussed terminology, which Lemkin had been thinking about since Churchill's "crime without a name" speech and the word he chose to describe it: genocide.

New conceptions require new terms. By "genocide" we mean the destruction of a nation or of an ethnic group. This new word, coined by the author to denote an old practice in its modern development, is made from the ancient Greek word *genos* (race, tribe) and the Latin *cide* (killing), thus corresponding in its formation to such words as tyrannicide, homocide, infanticide, etc. Generally speaking, genocide does not necessarily mean the immediate destruction of a nation, except when accomplished by mass killings of all members of a nation. It is intended rather to signify a coordinated plan of different actions aiming at the destruction of essential foundations of the life of national groups, with the aim of annihilating the groups themselves. The objectives of such a plan would be disintegration of the political and social institutions, of culture, language, national feelings, religion, and the economic existence of national groups, and the destruction of the personal security, liberty, health, dignity, and even the lives of the individuals belonging to such groups. Genocide is directed against the national group as an entity, and the actions involved are directed against individuals, not in their individual capacity, but as members of the national group.

The following illustration will suffice. The confiscation of property of nationals of an occupied area on the ground that they have left the country may be considered simply as a deprivation of their individual property rights. However, if the confiscations are ordered against individuals solely because they are Poles, Jews, or Czechs, then the same confiscations tend in effect to weaken the national entities of which those persons are members.[21]

BEYOND THE READING

Videotapes available for educators at the Facing History Lending Library are *Conspiracy* (2001) and *The Wannsee Conference* (1984).[22] These dramatized narratives depict the legal and bureaucratic groundwork laid by the Nazis in preparation for the extermination of the Jews.

A lesson plan entitled *Planning for Genocide: The Wannsee Conference* is available at the Facing History Online Campus (www.facinghistory.org/wannseelesson).

For more information about issues discussed in this reading, see the December issue of the 2005 *Journal of Genocide Studies*. The entire volume is devoted to Raphael Lemkin.

---

1 Raphael Lemkin, *Totally Unofficial Man: The Autobiography of Raphael Lemkin, in Pioneers of Genocide Studies*, ed. Steven L. Jacobs and Samuel Totten (New Brunswick: Transaction Books, 2002), 382.

2 Winston Churchill, *Never Give In! The Best of Winston Churchill's Speeches* (New York: Hyperion, 2003), 299-300.

3 Ibid., 300.

4 Lemkin, *Totally Unofficial Man*, 384.

5 Ibid., 383-84.

6 Ibid., 384.

7 Many of these terms are discussed in Henry R. Huttenbach, "Lemkin Redux: In Quest of a Word," *Journal of Genocide Research* 7 (December 2005): 443-45. The entire issue is devoted to Lemkin.

8 Geoffrey Robertson, *Crimes Against Humanity: The Struggle for Global Justice* (New York: The New Press, 1999), 1-16.

9 Brown University has recently produced a study of its historical ties with people who benefited from slavery. The report includes a succinct analysis of the development of the term crimes against humanity and related international laws. See Brown University Steering Committee on Slavery and Justice, *Slavery and Justice* (2006), 33-7. Brown University website, http://brown.edu/Research/Slavery_Justice/documents/SlaveryAndJustice.pdf (accessed November 13, 2006).

10 The Hague Conventions of 1899 and 1907 were one of the first attempts to create a body of international laws to regulate war. These agreements set rules for the commencement of war and for conduct of warring parties and neutral powers towards each other. It also outlawed the use of certain types of weapons in warfare and made set standards for the humane treatment of civilians during the time of war.

11 In 1945 the victorious powers of World War II defined the term more precisely in preparation for the Nuremberg trials: "Crimes against humanity: namely, murder, extermination, enslavement, deportation, and other inhuman acts committed against any civilian population, before or during the war; or persecutions on political, racial, or religious grounds in execution of or in connection with any crime within the jurisdiction of the Tribunal, whether or not in violation of the domestic law of the country where perpetrated." But even then the crime was limited to crimes committed during war.

12 Raphael Lemkin, "The New Word and the New Idea," Raphael Lemkin Papers, New York Public Library Rare Books and Manuscript Division, reel 3.

13 Raphael Lemkin, *Axis Rule in Occupied Europe: Laws of Occupation, Analysis of Government, Proposals for Redress* (Washington, DC: Carnegie Endowment for International Peace, 1944), 79.

14 Ibid. See also William A. Schabas, *Genocide in International Law: The Crimes of Crimes* (Cambridge: Cambridge University Press, 2000), 27.

15 Lemkin, *Axis Rule,* 79.

16 Raphael Lemkin, "Genocide," *American Scholar* 15 (April 1946), 228.

17 Letter to Mrs. Elizabeth Nowinski from G&C Merriam Company, Raphael Lemkin Papers, New York Public Library Rare Books and Manuscript Division, reel 1.

18 A. M. Rosenthal, "A Man Called Lemkin," *New York Times*, October 18, 1988. Rosenthal was a *New York Times* executive editor and worked for the newspaper for over fifty years.

19 Raphael Lemkin, "The Legal Case against Hitler," *The Nation*, February 24, 1945, 205.

20 Winston Churchill, *Never Give In! The Best of Winston Churchill's Speeches* (New York: Hyperion, 2003), 297-300.

21 Lemkin, *Axis Rule,* 79.

22 Frank Pierson, *Conspiracy*, VHS (New York: HBO Videos, 2001); Heinz Schirk, *The Wannsee Conference*, VHS (Los Angeles: Prism Entertainment, 1984).

Lemkin and the Nuremberg Trials

By spring 1945 the Allies (including British, French, Soviet Union, and American forces) had crushed the Nazi armies. In May World War II ended in Europe, and the grim details of Nazi atrocities spread across the world's headlines. As the camps were emptied, people everywhere saw photographs and news films of these sites of industrial mass murder, where some six million Jews had died alongside hundreds of thousands of members of other "undesirable" minorities. The Nazi crimes had been exposed.

Nordhausen concentration camp, Germany, April 1945. In the spring of 1945, the Allies liberated concentration camps and gathered evidence of genocide.

Credit: Image # 26811, This photograph is copyright of the USHMM.

Confronted by these unimaginable crimes, Allied leaders had to decide how to punish those who had planned and carried them out. Churchill and the premier of the Soviet Union Joseph Stalin, (as well as some members of American president Franklin Delano Roosevelt's administration) thought that as perpetrators of some of history's greatest war crimes, these men deserved immediate execution. They felt that holding trials would simply give the Nazi leaders an opportunity to defend their actions. Besides, hadn't their victims been denied trials of any kind?

But Roosevelt thought executions without trials would be unwise, and the United States was the first government to say that trials should be permitted for the Nazi leaders. The reasons for the American viewpoint had been stated before the end of the war by three members of Roosevelt's cabinet. Secretary of State Cordell Hull, Secretary of War Henry L. Stimson, and Secretary of the Navy James Forrestal had argued in favor of judicial proceedings that would "rest securely upon traditionally established legal concepts." They believed that using an approach based on laws would mean not only that "the guilty of this generation [will] be brought to justice," but that, "in addition, the conduct of the Axis

[Germany, Italy, and Japan] will have been solemnly condemned by an international adjudication of guilt that cannot fail to impress generations to come."[1] They also believed that a prosecution based on laws would set a precedent that would make any future such crimes clearly illegal. Their ideas reflected a bedrock belief that evil should be punished through laws agreed upon by society; to punish it by violent action taken in haste and without evaluation by impartial judges would be too much like what the Nazis had done.

At a conference in London in the summer of 1945, the other Allies (Great Britain, France, and the Soviet Union) agreed to the American proposal and created a charter for the first International Military Tribunal, which would be held in Nuremberg, Germany. This document defined three separate crimes that would be investigated: crimes against peace, war crimes, and crimes against humanity. Under the heading of war crimes were grouped the murder and ill treatment of civilian populations, deliberate and systematic persecution of ethnic groups, slave labor, the murder and ill treatment of prisoners of war, and the killing of hostages.[2]

The Nuremberg trials stood in stark contrast to the light treatment Mehmed Talaat and his subordinates had received after the massacre of the Armenians. Agreeing with Lemkin for the first time, the Allies publicly declared to the rest of the world that no nation had the right to kill millions of innocent people and that leaders who carried out such actions would be punished. Justice Robert H. Jackson, the lead American prosecutor at the trials, expressed this unique moment of agreement: the wrongs the Nazi defendants

Credit: Picker Art Gallery, Colgate University, gift of Yevgeny Khaldei

The accused bench, Nuremberg. Lemkin was an advisor to Robert Jackson, the Chief Council for the United States, during the Nuremberg trials.

had committed were "so calculated, so malignant, and so devastating, that civilization cannot tolerate their being ignored, because it cannot survive their being repeated."[3] The Allies' shared belief in this idea contributed enormously to the success of the trials, both in demonstrating the world's moral outrage and in punishing several of the top architects of the Nazi killing machine. The success of the trials created a precedent for future prosecution of similar crimes and laid the cornerstone on which contemporary international law was built.

Lemkin, who served as an adviser to Jackson, also worked behind the scenes to make sure that the crime of genocide was included in the charges against the Nazi leaders. His effort was successful. The third count of the indictment, which listed the war crimes of which the defendants were accused, said that they had "conducted deliberate and systematic genocide, viz., the extermination of racial and national groups, against the civilian populations of certain occupied territories in order to destroy particular races and classes of people and national, racial or religious groups, particularly Jews, Poles, and Gypsies and others."[4] Lemkin believed that by including genocide in the indictment, "the enormity of the Nazi crimes has been more accurately described."[5]

Lemkin's success was not complete. Although the new word was used in the indictments and in the closing arguments of the trial, genocide was still not identified as a separate, well-defined crime. Lemkin was also disturbed by the continued commitment of the United States, Britain, the Soviet Union, and France to the idea of state sovereignty; they did not question Germany's absolute authority over its internal affairs before the war. As Justice Jackson explained,

> [o]rdinarily we do not consider that the acts of a government toward its own citizens warrant our interference. . . . We think it is justifiable that we interfere or attempt to bring retribution to individuals or to states only because the concentration camps and the

deportations were in pursuance of a common plan or enterprise of making an unjust or illegal war in which we became involved. We see no other basis on which we are justified in reaching the atrocities that were committed inside Germany, under German law, or even in violation of German law, by authorities of the German state.[6]

This meant that legally all the crimes committed by Germany before the war were considered internal affairs. These crimes, carried out during the 1930s, included: the systematic discrimination against German Jews; the severe restrictions on the movements and family life of Jews; the destruction of their synagogues and cultural institutions; the looting and confiscation of their property and money; the mass arrests and murders of Jewish cultural and scholarly leaders; and other crimes that paved the way for the later mass murder of Jews during the war. William Schabas, an expert on international law, points out that "although there was frequent reference [during the trials] to the preparations for the war and for the Nazi atrocities committed in the early years of the Third Reich, no conviction was registered for any act committed prior to 1 September 1939."[7]

If only his proposal to the Madrid conference in 1933 had been accepted, Lemkin believed, a number of problems raised by the Nuremberg trials would have been prevented. First, the pre-1939 crimes would have been internationally recognized and prosecuted. Also, the objection raised by people during and after the trials—that the International Military Tribunal did not have legal grounds for trying the Nazis—would have been easily answered. Finally, Lemkin felt that the tribunal's charter had failed to provide a permanent law for the prosecution of international crimes.[8] At best, it had drawn up a special law to deal with the specific Nazi crimes. "In brief," Lemkin concluded, "the Allies decided in Nuremberg a case against a past Hitler, but refused to envisage future Hitlers."[9] Lemkin, however, may have underestimated his own achievement. Already in the Subsequent Nuremberg Proceedings, a series of smaller trials that followed the International Military Tribunals, genocide was used as a separate charge. In the trial of the German mobile killing unit (the *Einsatzgruppen*), United States prosecutor Benjamin B. Ferencz charged Nazi officers with the crime of genocide and went on to explain that genocide "is fundamentally different from the mere war crime in that it embraces systematic violations of fundamental human rights committed at any time against the nationals of any nation."[10] Based on Jackson's argument, Lemkin feared that had the Nazis kept their persecution of Jews and other minorities within Germany, they would not have been brought to trial.

CONNECTIONS

1. How could treaties such as the International Military Tribunal ensure that the Nazi crimes would never be repeated? Can law prevent genocide?

2. While many thought that the Nuremberg trials succeeded beyond all expectations in bringing Nazi war criminals to justice, Lemkin saw them as "only a fragmentary treatment of the problem."[11] Why did he think the value of the trials was limited?

3. Because the Allies did not want to undermine the principle of state sovereignty for their own reasons, crimes committed before Germany invaded Poland in September 1939 were excluded from the Nuremberg charges. Lemkin thought that this was wrong. What is the right balance between national and international authority when it comes to issues involving human rights? Who can protect individual rights when the government itself violates them?

4. Some people thought that the International Military Tribunal was a typical instance of "victor's justice" under which the powerful winners of the war decided what punishment the powerless losers should be given. They said that neither the court nor the laws it relied on had existed when the "alleged" crimes were committed. So they believed that the tribunal had neither the jurisdiction nor a basis in legal precedent to judge Nazi criminals. How do you imagine Lemkin would have responded to this criticism?

BEYOND THE READING

Facing History has held three conferences on the Nuremberg trials and justice after genocide. Teaching materials (including video clips, lesson plans, and scholarly papers) are available through the Facing History Lending Library. Lesson plans can be found on Facing History's Online Campus (http://www.facinghistory.org/campus/).

For a comprehensive view of the Nuremberg trials and related issues, see Chapter 9 of *Facing History and Ourselves:* *Holocaust and Human Behavior* at www.facinghistory.org/hhb9pdf.[12]

Available at the Lending Library is a new, 14-minute film entitled *Nuremberg Remembered* (2005).[13] The film vividly introduces the trials through the words of survivors, participants in the trials, and legal experts. Also available is a documentary film entitled *Nuremberg Trials* (1973). The film includes wartime footage, courtroom scenes, and legal analysis.[14]

1 Cordell Hull, Henry L. Stimson, and James Forrestal, "Draft Memorandum for the President (November 11, 1941)," in Michael R. Marrus, *The Nuremberg War Crimes Trial, 1945-46: A Documentary History* (Boston: Bedford/St. Martin's Press, 1997), 29.

2 "Charter of the International Military Tribunal," in Marrus, *The Nuremberg War Crimes Trial*, 52.

3 "Opening Statement before the International Military Tribunal," Robert H. Jackson Center website, http://www.roberthjackson.org/Man/theman2-7-8-1/ (accessed October 7, 2005).

4 Marrus, *Nuremberg War Crimes*, 65. Emphasis added.

5 Raphael Lemkin, "Genocide," *American Scholar* 15 (April 1946), 230.

6 Robert H. Jackson, "International Conference on Military Trials: London, 1945. Minutes of Conference Session, July 23, 1945", *The Avalon Project at Yale Law School* website, http://www.yale.edu/lawweb/avalon/imt/jackson/jack44.htm (accessed on January 26, 2005); cited in William Schabas, *Genocide*, 35.

7 William A. Schabas, "The 'Odious Scourge': Evolving Interpretations of the Crime of Genocide," *Genocide Studies and Prevention* 1, 2 (September 2006), 95.

8 Raphael Lemkin, "Genocide as a Crime under International Law," *American Journal of International Law* 41(1947), 146-48.

9 Raphael Lemkin, *Totally Unofficial Man: The Autobiography of Raphael Lemkin,* in *Pioneers of Genocide Studies*, ed. Steven L. Jacobs and Samuel Totten (New Brunswick: Transaction Books, 2002), 384.

10 Benjamin B. Ferencz, "Einsatzgruppen trial: U.S. prosecution condemns genocide (Nuremberg, September 29, 1947), United States Holocaust Memorial Museum website, http://www.ushmm.org/wlc/fi_fset.php?lang=en&ModuleId=10007138&ArticleId=5486&MediaId=184 (accessed October, 3, 2006).

11 Lemkin, *Totally Unofficial Man*, 368.

12 *Facing History and Ourselves: Holocaust and Human Behavior* (Brookline: Facing History and Ourselves, 1994).

13 Rebecca Richman Cohen, *Nuremberg Remembered*, DVD (Cambridge: Racing Horse Productions, 2005). The film was prepared for a Harvard Law School/Facing History and Ourselves conference held in November 2005 entitled Pursuing Human Dignity: The Legacies of Nuremberg for International Law, Human Rights, and Education.

14 Jack Kaufman, *Nuremberg Trials*, from *The Rise and Fall of the Third Reich*, VHS (Chicago: Films Incorporated, 1973).

Negotiating the Convention on the Prevention and Punishment of the Crime of Genocide

Humanitarian intervention—military action that is intended to protect victims of war crimes and genocides—was not new. In 1827 England, France, and Russia intervened to put a stop to atrocities committed during the Greek War of Independence. In 1840 the United States intervened on behalf of the Jews of Damascus and Rhodes; and the French attempted to stop religious persecution in Lebanon in 1861. Several efforts were also made to stop pogroms against the Jews and other minorities in Eastern Europe and the Ottoman Empire.

United Nations headquarters, Lake Success, New York. Lemkin tirelessly lobbied United Nations delegates to recognize genocide as an international crime.

Credit: Department of State, courtesy Harry S. Truman Library.

These attempts were carried out in the name of the international community. According to Leo Kuper's pioneering study of genocide, they showed that banning such crimes "had long been considered part of the law of nations."[1] Moreover, in 1915, when the massacre of thousands of Armenians in the Ottoman Empire was reported, France, Great Britain, and Russia declared that such acts constituted "crimes against humanity and civilization"—a definition that later played a crucial role in the Nuremberg trials (see Reading 4) and beyond. Yet Lemkin's vision went far beyond these earlier examples of international action. He argued that unless a permanent method of humanitarian intervention and of prosecuting genocidal criminals was established, all responses to genocide would be limited and unsatisfactory.

After the Nuremberg trials began, Lemkin traveled constantly from one international conference to another. He "buttonholed delegate after delegate. Always the answers were evasive. Genocide was an evil but what can be done about it?"[2] Exhausted and discouraged, Lemkin fell ill in Paris and checked himself into the American Military Hospital. As he lay in bed reading, a news item caught his attention: the United Nations, which had been created in 1945 to replace the League of Nations, was about to hold its inaugural meeting in Lake Success, New York (home of the United Nations in its first years).[3]

Ambassador Amado of Brazil (left) with Lemkin, 1948. Lemkin lobbied at the UN for the adoption of the Convention on the Prevention and Punishment of the Crime of Genocide.

Credit: UN Photo/MB/pj

Lemkin immediately left the hospital and rushed to catch a plane.

On arriving at Lake Success, Lemkin talked to every delegation that would listen, asking them to "enter into an international treaty which would formulate genocide as an international crime, providing for its prevention and punishment in time of peace and war."[4] During these months, Lemkin proved himself a relentless activist. While he was the main lobbyist for a United Nations' treaty to outlaw and prevent genocide, he did not act alone. He contacted many leading journalists and enlisted them to promote this idea. Prodding them with kind words and moral principles, he spread the word about his new idea. Lemkin also turned to other lobbyists for help. A number of nongovernmental organizations (NGOs)—organizations that are not funded by the state but by individuals who want to promote different causes—supported Lemkin's cause and helped him put pressure on United Nations delegates to promote it. Among these NGOs were the National Conference of Christians and Jews (one of the oldest human rights organizations in the United States, which recently changed its name to the National Conference for Community and Justice) and B'nai B'rith, a Jewish mass membership organization.[5] Tirelessly, he wrote innumerable pamphlets, petitions, newspaper articles, and personal letters to advance his idea. Lemkin was therefore a lobbyist, a strategist, and an agitator, all in one person.

Soon it became clear that two categories of nations were most likely to accept his ideas: those that were small and those whose continuing conflicts with powerful, aggressive neighbors made them want the protection a genocide law would offer. The first countries to endorse his proposal were Panama, India, and Cuba.

Next, Lemkin approached each delegation separately, explaining the details of what each nation had to gain from a discussion of genocide. He sent innumerable letters, sometimes pleading, sometimes flattering or scolding the delegates. Finally, on December 11, 1946, the General Assembly of the United Nations unanimously resolved that genocide was "an international crime and that a treaty should be drawn up" to punish those who carried it out.[6] Genocide would be defined as

> a denial of the right of existence of entire human groups, as homicide is the denial of the right to live of individual human beings; such denial of the right of existence shocks the conscience of mankind, results in great losses to humanity in the form of cultural and other contributions represented by these groups, and is contrary to the moral law and to the spirit and aims of the United Nations.[7]

Nearly two years of work by United Nations committees went by before the General Assembly met on December 9, 1948, in Paris to vote on the treaty that would become the Convention on the Prevention and Punishment of the Crime of Genocide (the Genocide Convention). One of Lemkin's biographers described the scene:

> The professor waited tensely in the Palais de Chaillot. For many years he had been working for this moment. After countless failures, the nations of the world were now ready to act on his plan. He listened intently as the roll was called, his heart beating faster and faster as he heard the delegates of nation after nation vote "Yes." Finally there were fifty-five votes in favor of the treaty.[8]

A storm of applause erupted in the hall. Hundreds of flashbulbs exploded in Lemkin's face. "The world was smiling and approving," Lemkin wrote, "and I had only one word in answer to all of that, 'Thanks.'"[9] And then, Lemkin wrote, all was calm.

The Assembly was over. Delegates shook hands hastily with one another and disappeared into the winter mists of Paris. The same night I went to bed with [a] fever. I was ill and bewildered. The following day I was in the hospital in Paris. . . . Nobody had established my diagnosis. I defined it. . .as Genociditis: exhaustion from the work on the Genocide Convention.[10]

A day later, on December 10, 1948, the Universal Declaration of Human Rights was adopted in another session of the General Assembly. The Genocide Convention and the declaration set new, universal standards for the treatment of individuals and groups in times of peace and war. While Lemkin had a number of reservations regarding the declaration, the two resolutions represented a rare moment of international unity and a focus on human rights.

The convention declared that "genocide is a crime under international law, contrary to the spirit and aims of the United Nations

---

The convention declared that "genocide is a crime under international law, contrary to the spirit and aims of the United Nations and condemned by the civilized world."

---

and condemned by the civilized world." [11] Lemkin had always believed that genocide should not be defined only as a war crime: in fact, the convention stated explicitly that it could occur "in time of peace or in time of war."[12] The treaty also reflected two of his other obsessions: first, the crime would be extraditable—that is, those who committed such crimes could not seek asylum or refuge in other countries; second, the definition of genocide would go beyond mass murder to include the "intent to destroy, in whole or in part," members of a specific group. (Article II decreed that included in the definition are all "acts committed with intent to destroy, in whole or in part, a national, ethnical, racial or religious group."[13] The decision not to include any mention of what he called "cultural genocide," the systematic destruction of a community's heritage, was, by comparison, a minor disappointment for him.

Article II of the treaty, which defined the kinds of groups that had to be protected by international law, had caused a good deal of discussion. Many members felt that political groups, as well as national, ethnic, racial, and religious groups, needed legal protections. No doubt this was true, especially at a time when the Soviet Union, under the leadership of Stalin, was conducting a political witch hunt that left millions dead or imprisoned. But the Soviet Union was not the only member nation to object to including political groups in the treaty:

❖ Several nations argued that the protection of political groups was a human rights issue that should be dealt with by the United Nations Human Rights Commission.

❖ Others (including Venezuela, Iran, and Egypt) argued that political groups were changeable and difficult to define; in addition, they could not easily be distinguished from groups of workers, artists, or scientists, which did not need international protection.

❖ Many countries in which civil unrest was going on threatened to pull out of the treaty if their governments could not oppose subversive political groups without risking accusations of genocide.[14]

Lemkin knew how damaging this debate could be to his cause. He used the term "political homicide" rather than "political genocide," and he argued against including any references to political groups. If he had not been able to persuade the opponents of the Soviet Union on this point, the Genocide Convention would certainly never have been approved.

Every nation that signed the convention would be obliged to try genocidal criminals either at home or in international tribunals. Article VIII called upon them to "take such action . . . as they consider appropriate for the prevention and the suppression of acts of genocide."[15] Although never legally used, Article VIII gave legal authority to the United Nations to fight crimes of genocide wherever they occurred. Article IX decreed that the International Court of Justice will allocate guilt and responsibilities of those who commit crimes of genocide. In the 1990s the clause was used to establish the International Criminal Tribunals for the former Yugoslavia and Rwanda—countries that experienced recent acts of genocide.

Officials who stood trial in these courts were often accused of genocide. In 1998 the permanent International Criminal Court (ICC) was established. The ICC's jurisdiction is over a list of the most important international crimes. Genocide is the first crime on that list.[16]

CONNECTIONS

1. What are international conventions? What is their role?

2. What is an activist? Was Lemkin an activist? Identify some of his arguments and tactics. Have you ever worked for a cause you thought important?

3. Why do you think many countries objected to broadening the terms of the Genocide Convention to include protections for political groups? Do you agree with Lemkin's decision to exclude them?

4. What tools did the convention make available to activists in their efforts to prevent genocide?

THE CONVENTION ON THE PREVENTION AND PUNISHMENT OF THE CRIME OF GENOCIDE

The Convention on the Prevention and Punishment of the Crime of Genocide was adopted by the United Nations General Assembly in December 1948. It went into effect in January 1951. The United States joined the convention in 1988. The text reflects Raphael Lemkin's ideas and tireless campaign to outlaw crimes of mass violence against minorities. For more information about this convention see Reading 4.

The Contracting Parties,

Having considered the declaration made by the General Assembly of the United Nations in its resolution 96 (I) dated 11 December 1946 that genocide is a crime under international law, contrary to the spirit and aims of the United Nations and condemned by the civilized world,

Recognizing that at all periods of history genocide has inflicted great losses on humanity, and

Being convinced that, in order to liberate mankind from such an odious scourge, international co-operation is required,

Hereby agree as hereinafter provided:

Article I

The Contracting Parties confirm that genocide, whether committed in time of peace or in time of war, is a crime under international law which they undertake to prevent and to punish.

Article II

In the present Convention, genocide means any of the following acts committed with intent to destroy, in whole or in part, a national, ethnical, racial or religious group, as such:

(a) Killing members of the group;

(b) Causing serious bodily or mental harm to members of the group;

(c) Deliberately inflicting on the group conditions of life calculated to bring about its physical destruction in whole or in part;

(d) Imposing measures intended to prevent births within the group;

(e) Forcibly transferring children of the group to another group.

Article III

The following acts shall be punishable:

(a) Genocide;

(b) Conspiracy to commit genocide;

(c) Direct and public incitement to commit genocide;

(d) Attempt to commit genocide;

(e) Complicity in genocide.

Article IV

Persons committing genocide or any of the other acts enumerated in article III shall be punished, whether they are constitutionally responsible rulers, public officials or private individuals.

Article V

The Contracting Parties undertake to enact, in accordance with their respective Constitutions, the necessary legislation to give effect to the provisions of the present Convention, and, in particular, to provide effective penalties for persons guilty of genocide or any of the other acts enumerated in article III.

Article VI

Persons charged with genocide or any of the other acts enumerated in article III shall be tried by a competent tribunal of the State in the territory of which the act was committed, or by such international penal tribunal as may have jurisdiction with respect to those Contracting Parties which shall have accepted its jurisdiction. . . .

Article VIII

Any Contracting Party may call upon the competent organs of the United Nations to take such action under the Charter of the United Nations as they consider appropriate for the prevention and suppression of acts of genocide or any of the other acts enumerated in article III.

Article IX

Disputes between the Contracting Parties relating to the interpretation, application or fulfillment of the present Convention, including those relating to the responsibility of a State for genocide or for any of the other acts enumerated in article III, shall be submitted to the International Court of Justice at the request of any of the parties to the dispute. [17]

BEYOND THE READING

For more teaching suggestions and additional information about the Universal Declaration of Human Rights, go to *Engaging the Future: Finding a Language for Peace* (www.facinghistory.org/engagingpeace), a Facing History reading that explores the role of Eleanor Roosevelt in the creation of the declaration.

To explore different aspects of the Universal Declaration of Human Rights, go to Facing History's lesson plan entitled *A World Made New: Human Rights after the Holocaust* (www.facinghistory.org/humanrightslesson).

1 Leo Kuper, *Genocide: Its Political Use in the Twentieth Century* (New York: Yale University Press, 1981), 19.

2 Robert Merrill Bartlett, *They Stand Invincible: Men Who Are Reshaping Our World* (New York: Thomas Y. Crowell Company, 1959), 103.

3 Information about the creation of the United Nations can be found in Dan Plesch, "The Hidden History of the United Nations," Open Democracy website, http://www.opendemocracy.net/debates/article.jsp?id=6&debateId=134&articleId=2519 (accessed December 31, 2005).

4 Raphael Lemkin, "Genocide," *American Scholar* 15 (April 1946), 230.

5 William Korey, *An Epitaph for Raphael Lemkin* (New York: The Jacob Blaustein Institute for the Advancement of Human Rights, 2001), 61-9.

6 Bartlett, *They Stand Invincible*, 104.

7 Lawrence J. LeBlanc, *The United States and the Genocide Convention* (Durham: Duke University Press, 1991), 23. The document quoted by LeBlanc is "General Assembly of the United Nations, Resolution 96 (I), December 11, 1946," United Nations website, http://daccessdds.un.org/doc/RESOLUTION/GEN/NR0/033/47/IMG/NR003347.pdf?OpenElement (accessed November 3, 2005).

8 Bartlett, *They Stand Invincible*, 105.

9 Raphael Lemkin, *Totally Unofficial Man: The Autobiography of Raphael Lemkin*, in *Pioneers of Genocide Studies*, ed. Steven L. Jacobs and Samuel Totten (New Brunswick: Transaction Books, 2002), 394.

10 Ibid., 395.

11 LeBlanc, *Genocide Convention*, 245-46. The document quoted by LeBlanc is the Convention on the Prevention and Punishment of the Crime of Genocide: General Assembly of the United Nations, Resolution 260A (III), December 9, 1948.

12 Ibid., 245.

13 Ibid.

14 Ibid., 61-3.

15 Ibid.

16 "Establishment of the International Criminal Court," United Nations website, http://www.un.org/law/icc/general/overview.htm (accessed on October 4, 2005).

17 Convention on the Prevention and Punishment of the Crime of Genocide, Prevent Genocide International website, http://www.preventgenocide.org/law/convention/text.htm (accessed on October 3, 2005).

International Law in the Age of Genocide

By October 14, 1950, twenty countries—the minimum needed—had ratified the Genocide Convention; ninety days later it went into effect. But serious problems lay ahead. As years stretched into decades, the nations whose support was needed for enforcement of the convention showed little interest in ratifying it. Among these, most notably, was the United States, which

Representatives from different states ratified the Convention in 1950. Seated (left to right): Dr. John P. Chang of Korea; Dr. Jean Price-Mars of Haiti; Assembly President, Ambassador Nasrollah Entezam of Iran; Ambassador Jean Chauvel of France; and Mr. Ruben Esquivel de la Guardia of Costa Rica. Standing, left to right: Dr. Ivan Kerno, assistant secretary-general for the department of legal affairs; Mr. Trygve Lie, secretary-general of the United Nations; Mr. Manuel A. Fournier Acuña of Costa Rica; and Dr. Raphael Lemkin, crusader of the Genocide Convention.

Credit: UN Photo/MB

was focused on its fear of Communism in the 1950s and then caught up in internal conflict over civil rights in the 1960s.

Why did these issues make many Americans think that their government should not support the convention? On June 16, 1949, President Truman transmitted the Genocide Convention for the Senate's approval (where such treaties are ratified). But soon a small group of senators blocked the process. Among them were Southern segregationists who believed in strict separation of Blacks and whites (or segregation). According to legal historian Lawrence LeBlanc, these Southern representatives asked, "[C]ould the convention be considered applicable to racial lynching?"[1] And if "mental harm" were considered genocide, segregation laws might also be considered genocidal.

Indeed, in 1951 the singer and civil rights activist Paul Robeson joined labor and civil rights activist William L. Patterson in a petition that accused America of genocidal treatment of its Black population. "We maintain," the petition read, "that the oppressed Negro citizens of the United States, segregated, discriminated against and long the target of violence, suffer from genocide as the result of consistent, conscious, unified policies of every branch of government."[2] In response, Lemkin claimed that segregation and genocide were separate crimes. Blurring the differences between the two, he added, played into the hands of those who were against American ratification of the convention.[3] In fact, opponents of the civil rights movement did use Robeson and Patterson's petition as "evidence" that the Genocide Convention would inflame the debate on civil rights in America.[4]

Other Americans feared that ratifying the convention would expose soldiers who had fought in the Korean War (and, later, the Vietnam War) to charges of genocide. The most outspoken critics of the convention felt that national sovereignty would be fatally weakened if American politicians, soldiers, and diplomats became subject to prosecution for genocidal acts.

Elements of antisemitism also crept into the statements made by those who opposed the treaty. Some directed hateful remarks against Lemkin, while others attacked the treaty precisely because it was designed (in their minds) to protect Jews and other minorities.[5] Many scholars say that while the vast majority of Americans supported the Genocide Convention, a handful of groups raised countless obstacles and managed to

delay the ratification process.[6] Sadly, a small number of representatives in the Senate (where international treaties required a two-thirds majority to pass) were able to block the ratification of the Genocide Convention for decades.[7]

In the meantime, Lemkin died. His longtime friend, *New York Times* editor A. M. Rosenthal, wrote that Lemkin died alone in a New York hotel "without medals or prizes." Only a handful of friends attended his funeral. Throughout his life, Rosenthal said, Lemkin "had no money, no office, no assistants. . . . He would bluff a little sometimes about pulling political levers, but he had none. All he had was himself, his briefcase, and the conviction burning

Credit: Wisconsin Historical Society, photo by *Milwaukee Journal Sentinel*, Image Whi-30142

William Proxmire (center) 1957. US Senator Proxmire gave 3,211 speeches about the Genocide Convention until the US ratified it.

in him."[8] Lemkin, in his own words, was a "totally unofficial man." Despite being nominated for the Nobel Peace Prize, his achievements were hardly recognized during his lifetime.

American ratification of the Genocide Convention had been a dead issue for almost a decade when William Proxmire, a senator from Wisconsin, got involved. Stunned by America's inaction on what he saw as a crucial issue, Proxmire made a remarkable decision. On January 11, 1967, he declared that "the Senate's failure to act [to ratify the Genocide Convention] has become a national shame. . . . I serve notice today that from now on I intend to speak day after day in this body to remind the Senate of our failure to act."[9] So whenever the Senate convened, there stood Wisconsin's senior senator, lecturing his colleagues.

But Proxmire underestimated the indifference of his fellow legislators; he also did not foresee how easily extremist groups would create widespread fear that under the convention, patriotic Americans would be tried for crimes of genocide. It took another 19 years and 3,211 speeches to persuade the Senate to adopt a resolution (with ample qualifications) ratifying the Genocide Convention. Two years later, in 1988, Congress confirmed the resolution.[10]

After the convention was ratified by the United States, however, not much else happened. Author and activist Samantha Power claims that many countries today continue to ignore the treaty's requirements. She says that in the 1990s, the United States ratification made "politicians ever more reluctant to use Lemkin's word, the 'g-word,' because the feeling was, in the US government, that it would oblige the United States to do things it was otherwise ill inclined to do."[11]

Despite the horrifying lessons of the Holocaust and the widespread, enthusiastic support for the convention around the world, human beings have continued to kill other human beings in numbers inconceivable to earlier generations. According to the International Association of Genocide Scholars, "In the 20th century, genocides and mass state murders have killed more people than have all wars."[12] Tens of millions have died since 1948, many of them victims of genocide. Examples include the Cambodian Genocide, Iraq's attacks on its Kurdish minority communities, the genocide in Bosnia, the Rwandan Genocide, and the genocide in western Sudan. The Genocide Convention was invoked for the first time in 2004, when the United States grew concerned enough about massive violence in Sudan, but to this date (early 2007), little has been done to stop the killings.

CONNECTIONS

1. Human rights activists often pay a high price of marginalization, frustration, and isolation. How effective can a single person be in advocating important causes? In what ways was Lemkin able to make a difference?

2. When Lemkin died, he was poor. He was not famous and had received no awards. How does one evaluate the success of Lemkin's lifelong effort? How would you measure activists' success if their achievements can only benefit future generations?

3. According to the International Association of Genocide Scholars, "In the 20th century, genocides and mass state murders have killed more people than have all wars." How would you explain this? What can be done to make sure this is not repeated in the 21st century? How can ordinary people build on Lemkin's legacy?

4. The international community has avoided the term genocide for fear that it would force countries to send troops, which is costly, politically contentious, and painful. But even now that the term was used to describe the killings in Darfur, very little has been done to stop them.[13] What keeps world powers from using the Genocide Convention to stop violence in places such as Sudan?

5. Lemkin struggled throughout the late 1930s and early 1940s to draw attention to the destruction of the Jews in Europe. In 2005 Nicholas D. Kristof, a journalist, faced the same challenge. He wrote many times about the massive destruction of human lives in Darfur and warned readers that the world was allowing this humanitarian crisis to become "a tolerable genocide."[14] What does Kristof mean when he says that the genocide in Darfur could become "tolerable"? What factors contribute to international indifference toward these killings? How can those who find this indifference "intolerable" express their moral outrage? What can be done to increase our sense of solidarity with victims of genocides that take place thousands of miles away?

6. In 1951 singer and civil rights activist Paul Robeson and the chief of the Civil Rights Congress, William L. Patterson, delivered a petition to United Nations representatives. Written by Patterson, the petition called on the delegates to apply a wider definition of the crime of genocide to the brutal treatment of Blacks in America.[15] Do you agree with this idea, or do you think Lemkin was right to object to the broader definition requested in the petition? What arguments might be made on either side of the debate?

TESTIMONY BY SENATOR WILLIAM PROXMIRE BEFORE THE SENATE FOREIGN RELATIONS COMMITTEE

In 1948, three years after World War II had ended and after the Nazi atrocities were fully revealed, the international community responded to Lemkin's pleas to outlaw the crime of genocide: In December, the newly formed United Nations adopted the Convention on the Prevention and Punishment of the Crime of Genocide.

The United Nations gave the convention its fullest support, and President Harry S. Truman signed it. But to Lemkin's bitter disappointment, the United States representatives refused to ratify (or approve) the treaty.

When Lemkin died in 1959, alone in a New York hotel, the Genocide Convention lost its greatest advocate. For almost a decade, the treaty was neglected and ignored. Then, in 1967, Wisconsin Senator William Proxmire decided to take on the challenge and he pledged to give a speech a day until the convention was adopted. 3,211 speeches later, the United States Senate adopted a ratification resolution (February 1986); Proxmire's "Genocide Convention Implementation Act" passed in 1987, and President Ronald Reagan signed it into law at the end of Proxmire's Senate career (November 4, 1988). The speech below conveys Proxmire's impassioned commitment to the cause of international laws and the Genocide Convention:

May 24, 1977

[T]he Genocide Convention has been pending before the Senate since President Truman first submitted it for ratification in 1949.

Think about that for a moment. 1949 to 1977. That's a full quarter century. An entire generation has been born and grown to adulthood during those years, and still the Senate has not acted. . . .

This morning I would like to briefly outline why I believe this Convention is so terribly important, why I have voiced my support for it almost every day on the floor of the Senate since our opening session in 1967, and review the further developments since your last hearings that make ratification this year urgent.

Mr. Chairman, there is no human rights treaty that has been subject to more detailed scrutiny and engendered more controversy than the Genocide Convention. Every line, every phrase, every syllable has been studied over and over.

What then is this treaty about that it warrants such attention?

Its purpose is quite clear. The Genocide Convention attempts to safeguard under international law the most fundamental human principle—the right to live.

It is that simple. It is that complex.

The treaty language attempts to prevent the destruction of a national, ethnic, racial or religious group by defining genocide, outlawing it, and establishing procedures for trying and punishing violators.

These are nice phrases. Grand abstract principles.

But let's face it: we are talking about the planned, premeditated murder or extermination of an entire group of people—the most vicious crime mankind can commit. . . .

Why do so many groups support ratification?

First and foremost, on moral grounds. The United States is the only major nation, except the People's Republic of China, that has not joined in condemning this heinous crime. In fact, all of our major NATO and SEATO allies have acceded to the treaty. We stand alone among free Western nations.

Second, our failure to ratify this treaty has been a constant source of embarrassment to us diplomatically that has puzzled our allies and delighted our enemies. During your 1970 hearings former U.S. Ambassador to the United Nations, Charles Yost, detailed the way this fact was smugly thrown in our diplomats' faces whenever we had protested gross violations of human rights in other nations. There is no logic in continuing to provide others with a club with which to hit us.

Third, our ratification will strengthen the development of international law in this crucial area of human rights. As you know, Mr. Chairman, the development of international law is a slow and tedious process, requiring the concurrence of all of the major powers. Our inaction impeded the development of these fundamental moral principles.

Fourth, as a party to the Convention we would be in a better position to use our moral influence to bear in specific cases where genocide is alleged. For example, State Department personnel have written me in the past and indicated that our efforts to halt the genocide that occurred during the Nigerian Civil War would have been far more effective had we been a party to the Convention. Instead we were viewed as moral hypocrites.

Fifth, U.S. ratification at this time will help to spur renewed interest in the treaty among the newly emergent nations of the world. . . .

Mr. Chairman, it is clear that the Genocide Convention is a moral document. It is a call for a higher standard of human conduct. It is not a panacea for injustice.

But in the same way that the Geneva Conventions for the Treatment of Prisoners of War have improved the treatment of prisoners of war, the Genocide Convention will also make an important step toward civilizing the affairs of nations.

In closing my testimony in 1970 I recalled the words of the late Chief Justice Earl Warren, who said, "we as a nation should have been the first to ratify the Genocide Convention."

My plea to this Committee and my colleagues in the Senate is: let us not be the last![16]

Teachers who wish to expand the discussion of genocide beyond the scope of this essay may find the following videotapes and clips useful:

On Bosnia, see John Zaritsky, *Romeo and Juliet in Sarajevo*, PBS's *Frontline*, VHS (Boston: WGBH Educational Foundation, 1994).

For more information on the situation in Darfur, Sudan, see the Facing History videotape on the work done by Rebecca Hamilton of the Genocide Intervention Network entitled *Ways of Responding to the Genocide in Darfur* (Brookline: Facing History and Ourselves, 2005).

Witnessing Darfur: Genocide Emergency (Washington, DC: United States Holocaust Memorial Museum, 2005) contains two short films about the conditions in Darfur. In *Darfur Eyewitness*, former US Marine Brian Steidle describes what he saw in Darfur with the African Union Monitoring Force. In *Staring Genocide in the Face*, Director of the Committee on Conscience, Jerry Fowler relates stories told by refugees in Darfur.

On the reluctance of the international community to stop the genocide that took place in Rwanda in 1994, see a discussion between Facing History and Ourselves Executive Director Margot Stern Strom and the former United Nations Force Commander in Rwanda, Retired Lieutenant General Roméo Dallaire of Canada.[17]

See also Mike Robinson, Ben Loeterman, and Steve Bradshaw, *Triumph of Evil*, PBS's *Frontline*, VHS (Boston: WGBH Educational Foundation, 1999). Produced on the fifth anniversary of the Rwandan Genocide, the documentary weaves together interviews with state officials and United Nations officials who reflect on their failure to address the events in 1994.

For additional information on the genocide in Rwanda, see Greg Barker, *Ghost of Rwanda*, PBS's *Frontline*, VHS (Boston: WGBH Educational Foundation, 2004). Produced 10 years after the genocide, the film examines the social, political, and diplomatic failures that led to the killings of close to one million Rwandans.

On the failed attempt of United Nations soldiers to protect Tutsi victims during the Rwandan Genocide, see *A Good Man in Hell: General Dallaire and the Rwandan Genocide*, VHS (Washington, DC: United States Holocaust Memorial Museum, 2002). This conversation between Ted Koppel and General Dallaire provides an overview of the genocide and discusses the moral dilemmas raised by foreign intervention.

1 Lawrence J. LeBlanc, *The United States and the Genocide Convention* (Durham: Duke University Press, 1991), 236.

2 William Patterson, *We Charge Genocide: The Crime of Government Against the Negro People* (New York: Civil Rights Congress, 1951), xi.

3 Raphael Lemkin, "Nature of Genocide," *New York Times*, June 14, 1953. See also "U.S. Accused in U.N. of Negro Genocide," *New York Times*, December 18, 1951; LeBlanc, *Genocide Convention*, 45.

4 Le Blanc, *Genocide Convention*, 35-49, William Korey, *An Epitaph for Raphael Lemkin* (New York: The Jacob Blaustein Institute for the Advancement of Human Rights, 2001), 60-2.

5 Samantha Power, *"A Problem from Hell": America and the Age of Genocide* (New York: Basic Books, 2002), 68, 72. Korey, *An Epitaph for Raphael Lemkin*, 67.

6 LeBlanc, *Genocide Convention*, 110.

7 William Korey, interview by Facing History and Ourselves, December 19, 2006.

8 A. M. Rosenthal, "A Man Called Lemkin," *New York Times*, October 18, 1988.

9 Power, *A Problem from Hell*, 79.

10 Ibid., 166.

11 Samantha Power, "A Problem from Hell: A Conversation with Samantha Power," Facing History and Ourselves website, http://www.facing.org/campus/reslib.nsf/all/4A339C1A6FECB82B8525718B004B06DE?Opendocument (accessed on December 29, 2005). This is a talk that Power gave on February 11, 2003 at an event sponsored by the Chicago Public Library and Facing History and Ourselves.

12 The Institute for the Study of Genocide and the International Association of Genocide Scholars, http://www.isg-iags.org/index.html (accessed on January 31, 2007).

13 *Rebecca Hamilton, Samantha Power: Ways to Respond to Genocide in Darfur*, VHS, (Brookline: Facing History and Ourselves, 2005). The videotape records a discussion of the genocide in Darfur held in November 2005 at a Harvard Law School/Facing History and Ourselves Program conference entitled Pursuing Human Dignity: The Legacies of Nuremberg for International Law, Human Rights, and Education (November, 2005).

14 Nicholas D. Kristof, "A Tolerable Genocide," *New York Times*, November 27, 2005.

15 For a further information on the petition read William L. Patterson, *We Charge Genocide: The Crime of Government against the Negro People* (New York: Civil Rights Congress, 1951).

16 William Proxmire, "Testimony before the Senate Foreign Relations Committee," May 24, 1977, Wisconsin Historical Society website, http://www.wisconsinhistory.org/turningpoints/search.asp?id=1512 (accessed on October 16, 2006).

17 2005 *New York Benefit Dinner*, VHS, (Brookline: Facing History and Ourselves, 2005).

About The Principal Publication Team

Series editor Adam Strom is the Director of Research and Development at Facing History and Ourselves. Mr. Strom is the principal author and editor of numerous Facing History publications that are distributed, in print and online, to educators across the globe.

Totally Unofficial: Raphael Lemkin and the Genocide Convention primary writer Dan Eshet received a doctoral degree in British history from the University of California, Los Angeles in 1999. He taught at a number of universities, including three years at Harvard's program on history and literature. Since 2005 Eshet has been working as a historian at Facing History and Ourselves.

The author of the introduction to *Totally Unofficial: Raphael Lemkin and the Genocide Convention*, Omer Bartov, teaches German and European history at Brown University and is considered a leading authority on the subject of genocide. He has written and edited numerous books on the Holocaust, war, and war crimes.

Lesson Plans Online

Facing History and Ourselves has developed a series of lessons that use materials from the case study *Totally Unofficial: Raphael Lemkin and the Genocide Convention* to help students learn about the origin of the term genocide, as well as to deepen students' understanding of political responses to mass violence. While these lessons were developed as a mini-unit, they could also be used independently.
For more, visit *www.facinghistory.org*.

About The Making History Series

The Making History Series of case studies is part of the *Choosing to Participate* initiative at Facing History and Ourselves and illustrates how citizens as individuals and groups across the world can choose to make a positive difference in society. The historically grounded case studies illuminate what the co-chair of the Facing History and Ourselves and Harvard Law School project Martha Minow calls the "levers of power"—the tools available to individuals and groups seeking to fight hatred, prevent genocide, and strengthen democracy. While civic education is often limited to instruction about the basic foundations of democratic governance, these case studies will reveal how the structures of civil society can be used by individuals and groups in their efforts to create positive change. Each case study will highlight the challenges and legacies of those who have struggled to promote human dignity, protect human rights, and cultivate and sustain democratic values.

FACING HISTORY & OURSELVES

Facing History and Ourselves is a nonprofit educational organization whose mission is to engage students of diverse backgrounds in an examination of racism, prejudice, and antisemitism in order to promote a more humane and informed citizenry. As the name Facing History and Ourselves implies, the organization helps teachers and their students make the essential connections between history and the moral choices they confront in their own lives by examining the development and lessons of the Holocaust and other examples of genocide and mass violence. It is a study that helps young people think critically about their own behavior and the effect that their actions have on the community, the nation, and the world. It is based on the belief that no classroom should exist in isolation. Facing History's programs and materials involve the entire community: students, parents, teachers, civic leaders, and other citizens.

Facing History provides educators with tools for teaching history and ethics, and for helping their students learn to combat prejudice with compassion, indifference with participation, and myth and misinformation with knowledge. Through significant higher education partnerships, Facing History also reaches and impacts new teachers before they enter their classrooms.

By studying the choices that led to momentous historical events, students learn how issues of identity and membership play out on the world stage. Facing History's resource books provide a meticulously researched yet flexible structure for examining complex events and ideas. Educators can select appropriate readings and draw on additional resources available online or from our comprehensive lending library.

Our foundational resource text, *Facing History and Ourselves: Holocaust and Human Behavior,* embodies a sequence of study that begins with identity—first individual identity and then group identities and definitions of membership. From there, the program examines the failure of democracy in Germany and the steps leading to the Holocaust: the most documented case of twentieth-century indifference, dehumanization, hatred, racism, antisemitism, and mass murder. It goes on to explore difficult questions of judgment, memory, legacy, and the necessity for responsible participation to prevent injustice. The book concludes with a section called "Choosing to Participate" that provides examples of individuals who have taken small steps to build just and inclusive communities and whose stories illuminate the courage, initiative, and compassion needed to protect democracy today and for generations to come. Other examples of collective violence such as the Armenian Genocide and the American civil rights movement expand and deepen the connection between history and the choices citizens face today and in the future.

Facing History's outreach is global, with a website accessed worldwide, online content delivery, a program for international fellows, and a set of nongovernmental organization (NGO) partnerships that allow for delivery of our resources in over 80 countries. By convening conferences of scholars, theologians, educators, and journalists, Facing History's materials are kept timely, relevant, and responsive to salient issues of global citizenship in the twenty-first century.

For more than 30 years, Facing History has challenged students to connect the complexities of the past to the moral and ethical issues of today. Students explore democratic values and consider what it means to exercise one's rights and responsibilities in the service of a more humane and compassionate world. They become aware that "little things are big"—seemingly minor decisions can have a major impact and change the course of history.

For more about Facing History, visit our website at *www.facinghistory.org*.

Printed in the USA
CPSIA information can be obtained
at www.ICGtesting.com
LVHW081302180923
758492LV00039BA/177

9 780983 787020